Contents

UNLEASHING THE MACHINE MIND: A BEGINNER'S GUIDE TO DEEP LEARNING CONCEPTS

DR.M.SIVAKUMAR

DR.P.SAVARIDASSAN

DR.N.KRISHNARAJ

DR.M.MARANCO

ONE
INTRODUCTION

In the realm of artificial intelligence, deep learning has emerged as a revolutionary force, capable of tasks once thought to be exclusively human. From recognizing images to understanding natural language, deep learning models are transforming industries and reshaping our world. This guide aims to provide a comprehensive yet accessible introduction to deep learning concepts. We will delve into the fundamental building blocks of neural networks, explore their diverse applications, and discuss the ethical considerations surrounding their development. By the end of this journey, you will have a solid understanding of deep learning and its potential to revolutionize various fields. Whether you are a seasoned data scientist or a curious beginner, this guide will equip you with the knowledge to embark on your own deep learning adventures. Let's dive in and unleash the machine mind!

Deep learning, a subset of machine learning, is characterized by its ability to learn from large amounts of data and extract complex patterns. It is inspired by the structure and function of the human brain, with artificial neural networks serving as the fundamental building blocks. These networks consist of interconnected layers of neurons, each responsible for processing and transmitting information.

One of the key advantages of deep learning is its ability to automatically learn features from raw data, eliminating the need for manual feature engineering. This has led to significant advancements in various domains, including computer vision, natural language processing, and speech recognition. For instance, deep learning models have achieved remarkable accuracy in tasks such as object detection, image classification, and machine translation.

However, the development and deployment of deep learning models also raise ethical concerns. Bias in training data can lead to discriminatory outcomes, and the privacy implications of collecting and processing large amounts of data must be carefully considered. It is essential to ensure that deep learning is developed and used responsibly, with transparency and accountability.

This book will explore the core concepts of deep learning, including neural network architectures, training algorithms, and evaluation metrics. We will also discuss practical applications and best practices for building and deploying deep learning models. By the end, you will be equipped with the knowledge and skills to harness the power of deep learning and contribute to the ongoing revolution in artificial intelligence.

TWO
INTRODUCTION TO DEEP LEARNING

What is Deep Learning?

Deep Learning is a subset of machine learning that involves training artificial neural networks to learn from large amounts of data. It's inspired by the structure and function of the human brain, where interconnected neurons work together to process information.

Key characteristics of Deep Learning:

Hierarchical Learning: Hierarchical learning is a crucial aspect of deep learning models that enables them to learn from multiple layers of abstraction. This multi-layered approach allows these models to identify complex patterns and features in data that would be difficult or impossible to detect using traditional machine learning methods. By extracting low-level features in the initial layers and combining them to form more complex features in subsequent layers, deep learning models can capture intricate relationships and patterns within data that are often difficult to represent using traditional techniques. This hierarchical structure not only improves the model's ability to learn complex patterns but also reduces the need for extensive feature engineering, making it a more efficient and effective approach to machine learning tasks.

Feature Learning: Feature Learning is a key advantage of deep learning models over traditional machine learning algorithms. Unlike traditional methods that require human experts to manually engineer features, deep learning models can automatically learn relevant features directly from the raw data. This eliminates the time-consuming and often error-prone process of feature engineering, allowing for more efficient and effective model development. Deep learning models achieve this by using hierarchical learning, where they extract low-level features in the initial layers and combine them to form more complex features in subsequent layers. This enables the model to discover hidden patterns and relationships within the data that might not be apparent to human experts.

Large Datasets: Large Datasets are crucial for training effective deep learning models. Deep learning algorithms learn from patterns in data, and the more data they have to analyze, the better they can identify and understand these patterns. This is especially true for complex tasks like image recognition, natural language processing, and speech recognition, which require models to learn from a vast amount of diverse data. However, the need for large datasets can also be a limitation, as it can be challenging to obtain and process such data, especially for specialized domains or rare events.

Neural Networks: Neural Networks are the fundamental building blocks of deep learning. They are inspired by the structure and function of the human brain, consisting of interconnected layers of artificial neurons. Each neuron receives inputs from the previous layer, processes them using a nonlinear activation function, and produces an output that is passed on to the next layer. This hierarchical structure allows neural networks to learn complex patterns and relationships within data, making them powerful tools for a wide range of applications, from image recognition to natural language processing.

Common types of neural networks used in deep learning:

Feedforward Neural Networks: Feedforward Neural Networks are the simplest type of neural network, where information flows in one direction from the input layer to the output layer. These networks are composed of multiple layers of neurons, with each layer connected to the previous layer. Feedforward networks are often used for classification and regression tasks, where the goal is to predict a specific output based on a given input. While they are relatively simple in structure, feedforward networks can be quite powerful when trained on large datasets and with appropriate architectures.

Convolutional Neural Networks (CNNs): Convolutional Neural Networks (CNNs) are a type of neural network specifically designed for processing spatial data such as images and videos. They are characterized by their use of convolutional layers, which apply filters to the input data to extract features. These filters are essentially small matrices that slide across the input image, detecting patterns and features at different locations. CNNs are particularly effective for tasks like image classification, object detection, and image segmentation, as they can automatically learn relevant features from raw image data without requiring manual feature engineering.

Recurrent Neural Networks (RNNs): Recurrent Neural Networks (RNNs) are a type of neural network designed to process sequential data, such as text, time series, and audio. Unlike feedforward networks, RNNs have feedback connections that allow them to maintain information about previous inputs, making them suitable for tasks that require understanding context and dependencies over time. This makes RNNs particularly effective for tasks like language modeling, machine translation, and speech recognition.

Deep learning has achieved remarkable success in various applications, including:

Image recognition: Image recognition is a field of artificial intelligence that focuses on identifying and classifying objects and scenes within images. This technology involves training computer models on vast datasets of images, enabling them to learn and recognize patterns, shapes, and textures. By analyzing the visual information in an image, these models can accurately identify objects such as animals, vehicles, and human faces, as well as categorize scenes like landscapes, cityscapes, and indoor environments. Image recognition has a wide range of applications, including autonomous vehicles, medical image analysis, security systems, and visual search engines.

Natural language processing: Natural language processing (NLP) is a branch of artificial intelligence that focuses on the interaction between computers and human (natural) languages. It involves teaching computers to understand, interpret, and generate human language in a way that is both meaningful and useful. NLP techniques are used to develop applications such as machine translation, sentiment analysis, chatbots, and text summarization. By analyzing the structure, syntax, and semantics of language, NLP models can extract information, answer questions, and even engage in conversations with humans.

Speech recognition: Speech recognition is a technology that enables computers to convert spoken language into written text. It involves training models on large datasets of audio recordings and corresponding transcripts, allowing them to learn the patterns and sounds associated with different words and phrases. Speech recognition systems can be used for a variety of applications, including voice-activated assistants, transcription services, and language learning tools. By accurately transcribing spoken language, these systems can make it easier for people to interact with computers and access information.

Recommendation systems: Recommendation systems are algorithms that suggest products, services, or content to users based on their preferences, behaviors, or past interactions. These systems use various techniques, such as collaborative filtering, content-based filtering, and hybrid approaches, to identify patterns and correlations in user data. By analyzing user preferences and historical data, recommendation systems can provide personalized recommendations that increase customer satisfaction and engagement. They are widely used in e-commerce, streaming platforms, social media, and other industries.

Medical image analysis: Medical image analysis is a subfield of artificial intelligence that focuses on analyzing medical images, such as X-rays, CT scans, MRIs, and ultrasounds, to aid in the diagnosis and treatment of diseases. By using computer algorithms to identify patterns, anomalies, and abnormalities within medical images, AI can assist healthcare professionals in detecting and diagnosing various conditions, including cancer, cardiovascular disease, and neurological disorders. Medical image analysis has the potential to improve diagnostic accuracy, speed up the detection of diseases, and enhance patient care.

In essence, deep learning is a powerful tool that enables machines to learn from data and perform tasks that were once thought to be exclusively human.

Deep Learning vs. Traditional Machine Learning

Deep learning and traditional machine learning are both subsets of artificial intelligence, but they differ in their approaches to learning and problem-solving.

Traditional Machine Learning

- **Manual Feature Engineering:** Requires human experts to identify and extract relevant features from data.
- **Simpler Models:** Often uses linear models or decision trees, which are less complex than deep learning models.
- **Smaller Datasets:** Can work effectively with smaller datasets compared to deep learning.
- **Limited Complexity:** Struggles with complex tasks that require learning from multiple levels of abstraction.

Deep Learning

- **Automatic Feature Learning:** Learns features directly from raw data, eliminating the need for manual feature engineering.

- **Complex Models:** Uses deep neural networks with multiple layers, capable of learning complex patterns.
- **Large Datasets:** Typically requires large amounts of data to train effectively.
- **High Complexity:** Can handle complex tasks that traditional machine learning struggles with, such as image recognition and natural language processing.

In summary, deep learning is particularly effective for tasks that involve complex patterns and large datasets, while traditional machine learning may be more suitable for simpler problems or when data is limited.

Key Components of a Neural Network

A neural network is a computational model inspired by the structure and function of the human brain. It consists of interconnected layers of artificial neurons, each processing and transmitting information. Here are the key components of a neural network:

1. Neurons

Input Neurons: These are the first layer of neurons in a neural network. They receive data from the external environment, such as images, text, or numerical values.

Hidden Neurons: Located between the input and output layers, hidden neurons process the information received from the input layer. They apply mathematical operations to the data, such as weighted sums and activation functions, to extract relevant features and patterns.

Output Neurons: The final layer of neurons in a neural network, output neurons produce the network's final output. They represent the network's predictions or decisions based on the processed information from the hidden layers.

The number and arrangement of these neurons in a neural network can vary depending on the specific task and complexity of the problem being solved.

2. Weights and Biases

Weights: These numerical values determine the strength or importance of the connections between neurons. A higher weight means that the input from one neuron has a greater influence on the output of another. During the training process, the weights are adjusted to optimize the network's performance by minimizing the error between the predicted output and the actual target output.

Biases:

Biases are numerical values that introduce a threshold for activation. They act as a constant offset that can shift the neuron's activation function. Biases help control the output of a neuron, allowing it to fire even when the weighted sum of its inputs is close to zero.

Together, weights and biases are the learnable parameters of a neural network. By adjusting these parameters, the network can learn complex patterns and relationships within the data and make accurate predictions.

3. Activation Functions

ReLU (Rectified Linear Unit): This is one of the most widely used activation functions. It returns the input if it's positive and zero otherwise. ReLU is computationally efficient and helps prevent the vanishing gradient problem, which can occur in deep networks.

Sigmoid: The sigmoid function maps input values to a range between 0 and 1. It's often used in output layers of classification tasks to represent probabilities. However, it can suffer from the vanishing gradient problem.

Tanh: Similar to the sigmoid function, tanh maps input values to a range between -1 and 1. It's often used in hidden layers of neural networks.

The choice of activation function can significantly impact a neural network's performance. Different activation functions may be more suitable for specific tasks or architectures.

4. Layers

Input Layer: This is the first layer of a neural network. It receives input data from the external environment and passes it on to the hidden layers. The input layer consists of neurons, each representing a feature or attribute of the input data.

Hidden Layers: Located between the input and output layers, hidden layers process the information received from the input layer. They extract relevant features and patterns from the data by applying non-linear transformations using activation functions. The number of hidden layers and neurons in each layer determines the network's capacity to learn complex relationships.

Output Layer: The final layer of a neural network, the output layer produces the network's final output. The number of neurons in the output layer depends on the specific task. For example, in a classification task, the output layer may have as many neurons as the number of possible classes.

The architecture of a neural network, including the number and arrangement of layers and neurons, can be customized to suit the specific problem being solved.

5. Training

Backpropagation: This is a supervised learning algorithm that is used to adjust the weights and biases of a neural network to minimize the error between the predicted output and the actual output. It works by calculating the gradient of the loss function with respect to the weights and biases, and then updating them in the opposite direction of the gradient.

Loss Function: A loss function measures the difference between the predicted output of a neural network and the actual target output. Different loss functions are used for different types of tasks, such as mean squared error (MSE) for regression and cross-entropy for classification.

Optimizer: An optimizer is an algorithm that updates the weights and biases of a neural network during training to minimize the loss function. Common optimizers include gradient descent, stochastic gradient descent (SGD), Adam, and RMSprop.

The choice of loss function and optimizer can significantly impact the training process and the performance of a neural network.

THREE
NEURAL NETWORKS

NEURAL NETWORKS

Types of Neural Networks

Neural networks can be categorized based on their architecture and the way they process information. Here are some common types:

1. Feedforward Neural Networks

- **Simple structure:** Information flows in one direction from input to output layers.
- **No feedback loops:** No connections between neurons in the same or previous layers.
- **Suitable for tasks:** Image classification, regression, and pattern recognition.

2. Convolutional Neural Networks (CNNs)

- **Spatial structure:** Designed for processing grid-like data, such as images and videos.
- **Convolutional layers:** Extract features by applying filters to the input data.

- **Pooling layers:** Downsize the feature maps to reduce computational cost.
- **Suitable for tasks:** Image recognition, object detection, and image segmentation.

3. Recurrent Neural Networks (RNNs)

- **Sequential data:** Designed to process sequential data, such as text, time series, and audio.
- **Feedback loops:** Connections between neurons in the same or previous layers, allowing the network to remember past information.
- **Variants:** Long Short-Term Memory (LSTM) and Gated Recurrent Unit (GRU) address the vanishing gradient problem.
- **Suitable for tasks:** Natural language processing, speech recognition, and time series analysis.

4. Autoencoders

- **Unsupervised learning:** Learn to reconstruct input data from a compressed representation.
- **Encoder-decoder architecture:** Encode input data into a lower-dimensional latent space and decode it back into the original space.
- **Applications:** Dimensionality reduction, image compression, and anomaly detection.

5. Generative Adversarial Networks (GANs)

- **Two-player game:** Compete between a generator and a discriminator.
- **Generator:** Creates new data samples.
- **Discriminator:** Evaluates the authenticity of the generated samples.

- **Applications:** Image generation, style transfer, and data augmentation.

6. Transformer Networks

- **Attention mechanism:** Allows the model to focus on different parts of the input data.
- **Self-attention:** Enables the model to relate different parts of the input sequence to each other.
- **Applications:** Natural language processing, machine translation, and text summarization.

Choosing the right type of neural network depends on the specific task and characteristics of the data. For example, CNNs are well-suited for image-related tasks, while RNNs are effective for sequential data. Understanding the strengths and limitations of each type can help you select the most appropriate architecture for your application.

Understanding Neurons and Activation Functions

Neurons

Neurons, or artificial neurons, are the fundamental building blocks of neural networks. They are inspired by the biological neurons found in the human brain. A neuron receives inputs, processes them, and produces an output.

Key components of a neuron:

Inputs: Inputs are the values that are received by a neuron from other neurons or from the input layer. These values can be real numbers, representing the activation of the connected neurons, or binary values (0 or 1). The neuron then processes these inputs using its activation function to produce its own output.

Weights: Weights are numerical values that determine the strength or importance of the connections between neurons and their inputs. A higher weight means that the input from a connected neuron has a greater influence on the output of the current neuron. During the training process, the weights are adjusted to optimize the network's performance by minimizing the error between the predicted output and the actual target output.

Bias: A bias is a constant value that shifts the activation function of a neuron. It acts as a threshold, allowing the neuron to fire even when the weighted sum of its inputs is close to zero. Biases help control the output of a neuron and can be adjusted during training to improve the network's performance.

Activation function: An activation function is a mathematical function that introduces non-linearity into a neural network and determines the output of a neuron. It takes the weighted sum of the neuron's inputs and biases as input and produces an output value. Common activation functions include ReLU (Rectified Linear Unit), sigmoid, and tanh. These functions help neural networks learn complex patterns and relationships within data.

The process of a neuron:

1. **Weighted sum:** The weighted sum of the inputs is calculated by multiplying each input value by its corresponding weight and then adding all the products together. This weighted sum represents the combined influence of the inputs on the neuron's output.
2. **Bias addition:** The bias is added to the weighted sum to introduce a threshold or offset for activation. This allows the neuron to fire even when the weighted sum of its inputs is close to zero. The bias term helps the neuron to learn more complex patterns and relationships within the data.
3. **Activation function:** The activation function is applied to the result of the weighted sum and bias addition to produce the neuron's output. This output value represents the activation of the neuron and is passed on to the next layer of the neural network.

Activation Functions

Activation functions introduce non-linearity into neural networks, allowing them to learn complex patterns. Here are some commonly used activation functions:

1. Sigmoid:

- Output range: 0 to 1
- S-shaped curve
- Used in older neural networks but less common today due to the vanishing gradient problem.

2. ReLU (Rectified Linear Unit):

- Output range: 0 to infinity
- Simple and computationally efficient
- Widely used in modern neural networks.

3. Tanh:

- Output range: -1 to 1
- Similar to sigmoid but with a wider range
- Less commonly used than ReLU.

4. Leaky ReLU:

- Addresses the dying ReLU problem by allowing a small positive slope for negative inputs.
- More robust than ReLU.

5. Swish:

- A self-gated activation function that combines the benefits of ReLU and sigmoid.
- Shown to improve performance in some cases.

Choosing the right activation function depends on the specific task and the architecture of the neural network. ReLU is often a good starting point, but experimentation with different activation functions can help optimize performance.

Backpropagation: How Neural Networks Learn

Backpropagation is a crucial algorithm used to train neural networks. It's a supervised learning method that adjusts the weights and biases of the network to minimize the error between the predicted output and the actual target output.

The backpropagation process involves the following steps:

Forward pass: The forward pass is the process of propagating input data through a neural network to obtain the predicted output. Here's a breakdown of the steps involved:

1. **Input data is fed into the neural network:** The input data is provided to the input layer of the neural network.
2. **The input data is propagated through the layers:** The input data is passed from the input layer to the hidden layers and eventually to the output layer. Each neuron in each layer calculates its weighted sum and applies its activation function to produce its output.
3. **The final output of the network is obtained:** The output of the final layer represents the predicted output of the neural network. This output can be used for various tasks, such as classification, regression, or generation.

Error calculation: The error calculation is a crucial step in training a neural network. Here's a breakdown of the process:

1. **The difference between the predicted output and the actual target output is calculated:** The loss function is used to quantify the difference between the predicted output of the neural network and the actual target output. Different loss functions are suitable for different types of tasks, such as mean squared error for regression and cross-entropy for classification.

The calculated error provides a measure of how well the neural network is performing and guides the optimization process.

Backward pass:

The backward pass is the process of updating the weights and biases of a neural network to minimize the error between the predicted output and the actual target output. Here's a breakdown of the steps involved:

1. **The error is propagated backward through the network, layer by layer:** The error calculated in the previous step is propagated backward through the network, starting from the output layer and moving towards the input layer.
2. **The gradients of the loss function with respect to the weights and biases are calculated:** The gradient of the loss function with respect to each weight and bias is calculated using the chain rule. These gradients represent the direction in which the weights and biases should be adjusted to reduce the error.
3. **The weights and biases are updated using gradient descent or a variant like Adam or RMSprop:** The calculated gradients are used to update the weights and biases using an optimization algorithm such as gradient descent, stochastic gradient descent (SGD), Adam, or RMSprop. These algorithms adjust the weights and biases in the direction that reduces the error.

The backward pass is repeated multiple times, with each iteration refining the weights and biases and improving the network's performance. This process is known as training the neural network.

FOUR

DEEP LEARNING APPLICATIONS

Image Recognition and Computer Vision

Image recognition and computer vision are closely related fields that involve teaching computers to understand and interpret visual information. While image recognition focuses on identifying specific objects or patterns within images, computer vision encompasses a broader range of tasks, including object detection, image segmentation, and scene understanding.

Key concepts in image recognition and computer vision:

Feature extraction: Feature extraction is a crucial step in image processing and computer vision. It involves identifying and extracting distinctive features within images that can be used for classification, recognition, or other tasks. These features can be based on various characteristics, such as edges, corners, shapes, textures, or color information.

Once the features are extracted, they can be used to represent the image in a more compact and informative way. This representation can then be fed into machine learning algorithms for tasks like object recognition, image classification, or image search.

Feature matching: Feature matching is a technique used to compare extracted features from different images to find similarities or differences. By comparing the features, it is possible to determine if two images contain the same objects or scenes.

Feature matching is used in various applications, including:

- **Image stitching:** Combining multiple images into a panoramic view.
- **Object tracking:** Tracking the movement of an object in a sequence of images.
- **Image registration:** Aligning images to correct for differences in perspective or scale.

There are several different feature matching algorithms, such as nearest neighbor, Euclidean distance, and feature descriptors like SIFT (Scale-Invariant Feature Transform) and SURF (Speeded-Up Robust Features). These algorithms calculate the similarity between features from different images and identify matching pairs.

Object detection: Object detection is a computer vision task that involves locating and identifying objects within an image or scene. It is a more complex task than image classification, which only involves categorizing the entire image.

Object detection algorithms typically involve two steps:

1. **Region proposal:** This step involves generating potential bounding boxes or regions of interest within the image where objects might be located.
2. **Object classification:** This step involves classifying the objects within the proposed regions using a classification model.

Object detection has a wide range of applications, including:

- **Autonomous vehicles:** Identifying pedestrians, vehicles, and other objects on the road.
- **Surveillance systems:** Detecting and tracking people or objects of interest.
- **Medical image analysis:** Identifying abnormalities or lesions within medical images.

There are several popular object detection algorithms, such as:

- **R-CNN (Region-based Convolutional Neural Network):** A classic approach that uses selective search to generate region proposals and a convolutional neural network (CNN) for classification.
- **Fast R-CNN:** An improved version of R-CNN that shares features between region proposals and classification, making it faster.
- **Faster R-CNN:** An even faster version of R-CNN that uses a Region Proposal Network (RPN) to generate region proposals.
- **YOLO (You Only Look Once):** A single-stage detector that predicts both bounding boxes and object classes directly from the image.
- **SSD (Single Shot MultiBox Detector):** Another single-stage detector that uses a series of default bounding boxes and predicts object classes and offsets for each box.

Image segmentation: Image segmentation is a computer vision task that involves dividing an image into different regions or segments based on their content. These regions can represent different objects, scenes, or areas of interest within the image.

Image segmentation is used in a variety of applications, including:

- **Medical image analysis:** Identifying organs, tumors, or other structures within medical images.
- **Autonomous vehicles:** Understanding the road scene and identifying obstacles.
- **Image editing:** Isolating objects or regions for manipulation or removal.
- **Content-based image retrieval:** Finding similar images based on their visual content.

There are several different techniques for image segmentation, including:

- **Thresholding:** Dividing an image into foreground and background regions based on a threshold value.
- **Edge detection:** Identifying boundaries between different regions in an image.
- **Region-based methods:** Grouping pixels together based on their similarity in terms of color, texture, or other features.
- **Deep learning methods:** Using convolutional neural networks (CNNs) to learn features and segment images.

The choice of segmentation technique depends on the specific application and the characteristics of the images being processed.

Scene understanding: Scene understanding is a higher-level computer vision task that involves interpreting the overall context of an image, going beyond simply identifying individual objects. It aims to understand the relationships between objects, the environment in which they are located, and the overall scene.

Here are some key aspects of scene understanding:

- **Object recognition:** Identifying individual objects within the image.
- **Object relationships:** Understanding the spatial relationships between objects, such as proximity, occlusion, or containment.
- **Scene context:** Recognizing the overall environment or setting of the image, such as a street, a park, or a building.
- **Semantic understanding:** Interpreting the meaning or purpose of the scene, such as a person riding a bike or a group of people having a picnic.

Scene understanding is a challenging task that requires combining techniques from object detection, image segmentation, and natural language processing. It has applications in various fields, including autonomous vehicles, robotics, and augmented reality.

Applications of image recognition and computer vision:

- **Medical imaging:** Diagnosing diseases from X-rays, MRI scans, and other medical images.
- **Autonomous vehicles:** Enabling cars to perceive their surroundings and navigate safely.
- **Facial recognition:** Identifying individuals based on their facial features.
- **Retail:** Analyzing customer behavior and optimizing store layouts.
- **Manufacturing:** Inspecting products for defects and quality control.
- **Security:** Detecting and tracking objects in surveillance footage.

Deep learning and computer vision:

Deep learning has revolutionized the field of computer vision, enabling significant advancements in image recognition and related tasks. Convolutional Neural Networks (CNNs) are particularly well-suited for processing image data and extracting meaningful features.

Some popular deep learning architectures for computer vision:

AlexNet: AlexNet was a pioneering deep learning model that revolutionized the field of computer vision. Introduced in 2012, it featured a deeper network architecture with eight layers, including five convolutional layers and three fully connected layers, surpassing previous methods in terms of depth. This innovative approach, combined with the use of ReLU activation functions and GPU acceleration, enabled AlexNet to achieve groundbreaking performance in the ImageNet Large Scale Visual Recognition Challenge (ILSVRC). Its success demonstrated the power of deep learning for image recognition tasks and inspired the development of numerous subsequent models, solidifying its place as a cornerstone in the history of computer vision.

VGGNet: VGGNet is a deep convolutional neural network (CNN) architecture that builds upon the success of AlexNet. It is characterized by its use of multiple convolutional layers with small 3x3 filters, stacked in a sequence. This design choice allows for greater depth without significantly increasing the number of parameters. VGGNet also introduces the concept of a "very deep" network, demonstrating that deeper architectures can lead to improved performance. The VGGNet architecture has been influential in the field of computer vision, serving as a benchmark and inspiring subsequent models.

ResNet: ResNet (Residual Network) is a deep learning architecture that addresses the vanishing gradient problem, which can hinder the training of very deep networks. ResNet introduces residual connections, which allow information to skip layers and directly contribute to the output. These connections help to preserve gradients and enable the training of significantly deeper networks without suffering from performance degradation. ResNet has achieved state-of-the-art results on various tasks, including image classification, object detection, and image segmentation, demonstrating the effectiveness of its residual learning approach.

InceptionNet: InceptionNet is a deep learning architecture that employs a novel approach to feature extraction. Unlike traditional CNNs that use a single filter size, InceptionNet incorporates a mixture of different-sized convolutions (1x1, 3x3, and 5x5) within a single layer. This allows the network to capture features at multiple scales, improving its ability to recognize objects of varying sizes and shapes. InceptionNet also utilizes 1x1 convolutions to reduce the dimensionality of feature maps, making the network more computationally efficient. This innovative design has led to significant improvements in performance on various tasks, making InceptionNet a popular choice for computer vision applications.

By leveraging deep learning techniques, computer vision systems can achieve remarkable accuracy and performance in a wide range of applications.

Natural Language Processing (NLP)

Natural Language Processing (NLP) is a subfield of artificial intelligence that deals with the interaction between computers and human (natural) languages. It involves teaching computers to understand, interpret, and generate human language.

Key tasks in NLP:

Text classification: Text classification is a fundamental task in natural language processing (NLP) that involves automatically assigning text documents to predefined categories. This process is essential for various applications, such as email filtering, sentiment analysis, topic modeling, and document organization. By analyzing the content of a text document, classification algorithms can determine its most relevant category, enabling efficient information management and retrieval. Techniques like bag-of-words, TF-IDF, and machine learning algorithms are commonly employed to achieve accurate text classification, with advancements in NLP leading to continuous improvements in this area.

Named entity recognition: Named entity recognition (NER) is a subtask of natural language processing (NLP) that involves identifying and classifying named entities within text. These entities can include people, organizations, locations, dates, times, and other specific references. NER is a crucial component of many NLP applications, such as information extraction, question answering, and machine translation. By accurately identifying named entities, we can gain valuable insights from text data and improve our understanding of the world.

Sentiment analysis: Sentiment analysis, also known as opinion mining, is a subfield of natural language processing (NLP) that aims to identify and classify the sentiment expressed in a piece of text. This involves determining whether the text conveys a positive, negative, or neutral opinion. Sentiment analysis has applications in various domains, including social media monitoring, market research, customer service, and political analysis. By understanding the sentiment behind text data, we can gain valuable insights into public opinion, consumer behavior, and trends.

Machine translation: Machine translation is a subfield of natural language processing (NLP) that focuses on automatically translating text from one language to another. This technology leverages computational techniques to analyze and understand the source language, and then generates equivalent text in the target language. Machine translation has seen significant advancements in recent years, with deep learning models achieving impressive results on various language pairs. However, it's important to note that machine translation is not perfect and may still produce errors or inaccuracies, especially for complex or nuanced texts.

Question answering: Question answering is a subfield of natural language processing (NLP) that focuses on automatically answering questions posed in natural language. This involves understanding the question, retrieving relevant information from a knowledge base or text corpus, and generating a comprehensive and informative answer. Question answering systems have applications in various domains, such as customer support, search engines, and educational tools. By providing accurate and relevant answers to user queries, question answering systems can enhance user experience and improve access to information.

Text summarization: Text summarization is a subfield of natural language processing (NLP) that involves automatically creating concise summaries of longer texts. This involves identifying the most important information in the original text and condensing it into a shorter, coherent summary. Text summarization has applications in various domains, such as news aggregation, research paper summarization, and document retrieval. By providing summaries of lengthy texts, text summarization can save time and effort for users who need to quickly grasp the key points of a document.

Techniques used in NLP:

Tokenization: Tokenization is a fundamental preprocessing step in natural language processing (NLP) that involves breaking down text into individual words or tokens. This process is essential for various NLP tasks, such as text classification, named entity recognition, machine translation, and sentiment analysis. By identifying the boundaries between words and other elements in a text, tokenization enables the extraction of meaningful information and prepares the data for further analysis. However, tokenization can be challenging in languages with complex morphology or ambiguous word boundaries, requiring sophisticated techniques to achieve accurate results.

Stemming and lemmatization: Stemming and lemmatization are two techniques used in natural language processing (NLP) to reduce words to their root form, also known as the lemma. This process is essential for tasks like text classification, information retrieval, and topic modeling, as it helps to normalize text and improve the accuracy of analysis. Stemming is a simpler approach that involves removing suffixes or prefixes from words, while lemmatization is a more sophisticated technique that considers the morphological structure of words and uses a dictionary or lexicon to find the correct lemma. Both techniques can be beneficial in reducing the dimensionality of the data and improving the performance of NLP models.

Part-of-speech tagging: Part-of-speech tagging is a fundamental task in natural language processing (NLP) that involves identifying the grammatical category of each word in a sentence. This information is crucial for understanding the structure and meaning of text, and it is used as a preprocessing step for many NLP tasks. By accurately tagging words with their corresponding part-of-speech, we can gain insights into the syntactic structure of sentences, identify named entities, and improve the performance of tasks such as machine translation and sentiment analysis.

Dependency parsing: Dependency parsing is a subfield of natural language processing (NLP) that focuses on analyzing the grammatical structure of a sentence by identifying the dependencies between words. This involves determining the syntactic relationships between words, such as subject-verb relationships, object-verb relationships, and modifier-head relationships. Dependency parsing is essential for understanding the underlying structure of sentences and is used as a preprocessing step for many NLP tasks, including machine translation, question answering, and text summarization. By accurately parsing the dependency structure of a sentence, we can gain insights into the meaning and context of the text and improve the performance of

NLP applications.

Word embeddings: Word embeddings are a powerful technique in natural language processing (NLP) that represents words as numerical vectors, capturing the semantic relationships between them. These vectors are learned from large datasets of text and encode information about the context in which words appear. Word embeddings can be used to improve the performance of various NLP tasks, such as text classification, machine translation, and question answering. By representing words as dense, low-dimensional vectors, word embeddings allow NLP models to better understand the meaning and relationships between words, leading to more accurate and robust results.

Recurrent Neural Networks (RNNs): Recurrent Neural Networks (RNNs) are a type of neural network architecture specifically designed to process sequential data, such as text, time series data, and audio signals. Unlike traditional feedforward neural networks, RNNs have internal memory, allowing them to retain information from previous inputs. This ability makes RNNs well-suited for tasks that require understanding context and dependencies between elements in a sequence. RNNs are commonly used in natural language processing applications like machine translation, sentiment analysis, and text generation, where capturing the sequential nature of language is essential.

Transformer models: Transformer models are a type of neural network architecture that have revolutionized the field of natural language processing (NLP). Unlike RNNs, which process text sequentially, transformers use attention mechanisms to capture long-range dependencies between words in a sentence. This allows transformers to efficiently process text and understand the relationships between words that are far apart from each other. Transformer models have achieved state-of-the-art results on various NLP tasks, including machine translation, text summarization, and question answering. The success of transformer models has led to their widespread adoption in the NLP community.

Applications of NLP:

Chatbots and virtual assistants: Chatbots and virtual assistants are AI-powered applications that can simulate human conversation and interact with users through text or voice. They are widely used to provide customer support, answer questions, and perform various tasks. By leveraging natural language processing and machine learning, chatbots and virtual assistants can understand and respond to user queries in a natural and informative manner. They can be deployed on websites, messaging platforms, and even smart devices, offering convenient and efficient assistance to users.

Search engines: Search engines are powerful tools that enable users to find information on the vast expanse of the internet. By understanding user queries and analyzing the content of web pages, search engines can return relevant results that match the user's intent. This process involves complex algorithms that consider factors such as keyword matching, relevance scoring, and user behavior to deliver the most useful and informative results. Search engines have become an essential part of our daily lives, providing access to a wealth of knowledge and resources.

Language translation: Language translation is the process of converting text or speech from one language to another. It involves understanding the source language, analyzing its meaning, and generating equivalent text or speech in the target language. Language translation has applications in various fields, including business, education, travel, and diplomacy. Advancements in natural language processing and machine learning have led to significant improvements in language translation technology, enabling more accurate and fluent translations. However, it's important to note that machine translation is not perfect and may still require human intervention for complex or nuanced texts.

Text summarization: Text summarization is a subfield of natural language processing (NLP) that involves automatically generating concise summaries of longer texts. This process involves identifying the most important information in the original text and condensing it into a shorter, coherent summary. Text summarization has applications in various domains, such as news aggregation, research paper summarization, and document retrieval. By providing summaries of lengthy texts, text summarization can save time and effort for users who need to quickly grasp the key points of a document. Advancements in NLP techniques, including deep learning models and attention mechanisms, have led to significant improvements in text summarization, enabling the generation of more accurate and informative summaries.

Sentiment analysis: Sentiment analysis, also known as opinion mining, is a subfield of natural language processing (NLP) that involves identifying and classifying the sentiment expressed in text data. This technique is widely used to analyze customer feedback, social media sentiment, and public opinion. By understanding the sentiment behind text data, businesses can gain valuable insights into customer satisfaction, brand perception, and market trends. Sentiment analysis can be applied to a variety of sources, including reviews, surveys, social media posts, and news articles, providing valuable information for decision-making and customer engagement.

Information extraction: Information extraction is a subfield of natural language processing (NLP) that focuses on identifying and extracting specific pieces of information from text documents. This involves using techniques like named entity recognition, relationship extraction, and event extraction to locate and extract relevant data points. Information extraction is essential for various applications, including knowledge graph construction, customer relationship management (CRM), and business intelligence. By automating the process of extracting information from text, businesses can save time and resources, improve decision-making, and gain valuable insights from their data.

NLP has made significant progress in recent years, thanks to advancements in deep learning and the availability of large datasets. As NLP technology continues to evolve, we can expect to see even more sophisticated and natural-sounding language interactions between humans and machines.

Recommendation Systems

Recommendation systems are algorithms that suggest items or content to users based on their preferences, behaviors, or interactions with other users. They are widely used in various industries, including e-commerce, streaming services, social media, and content creation.

Types of recommendation systems:

Collaborative filtering: Collaborative filtering is a popular recommendation algorithm used in various applications, including e-commerce, music streaming, and social media. It works by analyzing user behavior or item attributes to suggest items that are likely to be of interest.

Here's a breakdown of the two main types of collaborative filtering:

- **User-based collaborative filtering**: This approach suggests items based on the preferences of similar users. It identifies users with similar tastes and recommends items that those users have liked or purchased. For example, if you often buy books by a particular author, a user-based collaborative filtering system might recommend other books by the same author or books by similar authors.

- **Item-based collaborative filtering**: This approach suggests items based on their similarity to items that the user has interacted with. It identifies items with similar attributes or content and recommends those that are likely to be of interest to the user. For example, if you have purchased a smartphone, an item-based collaborative filtering system might recommend accessories or cases that are compatible with that smartphone.

Both user-based and item-based collaborative filtering can be effective recommendation algorithms, and the best approach may vary depending on the specific application and dataset.

Content-based filtering: Content-based filtering is another popular recommendation algorithm that suggests items based on their attributes or features. It analyzes the content of items, such as text descriptions, tags, or keywords, and matches them to the user's preferences.

Here's a more detailed explanation:

- **Content analysis**: Content-based filtering systems extract information from items and represent them as numerical vectors. These vectors can be based on various features, such as keywords, topics, genres, or other relevant attributes.
- **User profiles**: User profiles are created based on their preferences or past behavior. These profiles can be constructed using information such as ratings, purchases, or interactions with items.
- **Matching**: The system compares the user's profile to the content vectors of items and recommends items that have the highest similarity or match the user's preferences.

Content-based filtering is particularly effective for recommending items with explicit content, such as movies, books, or music. It can also be used to personalize content on websites and social media platforms. However, content-based filtering can be limited by the availability of item features and may not be able to capture the diversity of user preferences.

Hybrid recommendation systems: Hybrid recommendation systems combine collaborative filtering and content-based filtering to leverage the strengths of both approaches. This combination can often lead to more accurate and personalized recommendations.

Here's a breakdown of how hybrid recommendation systems work:

- **Collaborative filtering**: This component analyzes user behavior or item attributes to suggest items based on similarities between users or items.

- **Content-based filtering:** This component analyzes the content of items and matches them to the user's preferences.
- **Combination:** Hybrid systems can combine these two approaches in various ways, such as:

  - **Weighted combination:** Assign weights to collaborative filtering and content-based filtering based on their relative importance.
  - **Switches:** Use collaborative filtering for users with a history of interactions and content-based filtering for new users or items with limited interaction data.
  - **Side information:** Incorporate additional information, such as social connections or demographics, to enhance the recommendations.

Hybrid recommendation systems can provide more accurate and personalized recommendations by considering both user behavior and item content. They can also address the limitations of individual approaches, such as the cold-start problem (when there is limited data for new users or items) or the risk of recommending overly similar items.

Key techniques used in recommendation systems:
Matrix Factorization:

- **Latent Factors:** Matrix factorization decomposes a user-item rating matrix into two smaller matrices, representing user and item latent factors. These latent factors capture the underlying preferences and characteristics of users and items.
- **Collaborative Filtering:** Matrix factorization is a popular technique for collaborative filtering, where recommendations are based on similarities between users or items.

Neighborhood-Based Methods:

- **User-Based or Item-Based:** Neighborhood-based methods find similar users or items based on their ratings or preferences. For example, user-based collaborative filtering recommends items that similar users have liked, while item-based collaborative filtering recommends items that are similar to those the user has interacted with.

Graph-Based Methods:

- **Modeling Interactions:** Graph-based methods model user-item interactions as a graph, where users and items are represented as nodes and connections between them represent interactions. Graph algorithms can then be used to make recommendations based on the graph structure.

Deep Learning Models:

- **Complex Patterns:** Deep learning models, such as neural networks, can learn complex patterns and relationships between users and items. This can lead to more accurate and personalized recommendations.
- **Hybrid Approaches:** Deep learning models can be combined with other techniques, such as matrix factorization and neighborhood-based methods, to create hybrid recommendation systems.

By understanding these key techniques, you can choose the most appropriate approach for your specific recommendation system based on the dataset, computational resources, and desired level of accuracy.

Challenges and considerations in recommendation systems:
Cold-Start Problem:

- **Limited Data:** The cold-start problem arises when there is limited or no data available for new users or new items. This makes it difficult to generate accurate recommendations.

- **Addressing the Problem:** To address the cold-start problem, techniques such as content-based filtering, collaborative filtering based on similar users or items, and hybrid approaches can be used.

Scalability:

- **Large Datasets:** Recommendation systems often deal with large datasets, which can pose scalability challenges. Efficient algorithms and distributed systems are required to handle such large-scale computations.
- **Real-time Recommendations:** In many applications, recommendations need to be generated in real-time, which further emphasizes the need for scalable solutions.

Serendipity:

- **Unexpected Recommendations:** Recommending unexpected but relevant items can enhance user satisfaction and discovery. This requires understanding user preferences and exploring diverse item spaces.
- **Serendipity Techniques:** Techniques such as exploring long-tail items, incorporating diversity constraints, and using serendipity-based algorithms can help to address this challenge.

Diversity:

- **Avoiding Overly Similar Recommendations:** Ensuring that recommendations are not overly similar is important to prevent users from getting bored or missing out on relevant items.
- **Diversity Metrics:** Using diversity metrics to evaluate the diversity of recommendations can help to address this challenge.

Ethical Considerations:

- **Bias and Fairness:** Recommendation systems should be designed to avoid biases and ensure fair treatment of users. This includes addressing issues such as filter bubbles and algorithmic bias.
- **Privacy:** Protecting user privacy is essential in recommendation systems. Techniques such as differential privacy and anonymization can be used to protect user data.

By carefully considering these challenges and addressing them through appropriate techniques, recommendation systems can provide valuable and personalized recommendations to users.

Applications of recommendation systems:

E-commerce:

- **Personalized Recommendations:** E-commerce platforms use recommendation systems to suggest products to customers based on their purchase history, browsing behavior, and other relevant factors. This helps to increase customer satisfaction and drive sales.

Streaming Services:

- **Content Discovery:** Streaming services like Netflix and Spotify use recommendation systems to suggest movies, TV shows, or music based on users' viewing history, ratings, and preferences. This helps users discover new content and enhances their experience.

Social Media:

- **User Engagement:** Social media platforms use recommendation systems to suggest friends, groups, or content to follow. This helps to improve user engagement and keep users on the platform.

Content Creation:

- **Topic Suggestions:** Recommendation systems can be used to suggest topics or articles to writers based on user interest. This can help to ensure that the content created is relevant and engaging to the target audience.

Personalized Advertising:

- **Targeted Ads:** Recommendation systems can be used to target ads to specific users based on their preferences, demographics, and browsing behavior. This can improve the effectiveness of advertising campaigns and increase ROI.

These are just a few examples of how recommendation systems are used in various industries. As AI continues to advance, we can expect to see even more innovative applications of recommendation systems in the future. Recommendation systems have become an essential component of many online services, providing personalized experiences and driving user engagement. As technology continues to advance, we can expect to see even more sophisticated and effective recommendation systems in the future.

Generative Models: Creating New Data

Generative models are a class of machine learning algorithms capable of generating new data samples that resemble the training data. They are used in various applications, including image and video generation, natural language generation, and drug discovery.

Two prominent types of generative models:

1. Generative Adversarial Networks (GANs):

- **Competitive framework:** GANs consist of two neural networks: a generator and a discriminator.
- **Generator:** Creates new data samples.
- **Discriminator:** Evaluates the authenticity of the generated samples.
- **Training process:** The generator and discriminator compete in a game, with the generator trying to fool the discriminator and the

discriminator trying to distinguish real from fake data.

- **Applications:** Image generation, style transfer, and data augmentation.

2. Variational Autoencoders (VAEs):

- **Probabilistic model:** VAEs are based on probabilistic modeling, using latent variables to represent the underlying structure of the data.
- **Encoder-decoder architecture:** The encoder maps input data to a latent space, and the decoder reconstructs the input data from the latent representation.
- **Regularization:** VAEs use a regularization term to ensure that the latent space is well-structured and can generate diverse samples.
- **Applications:** Image generation, data imputation, and anomaly detection.

Other generative models:

- **Flow-based models:** Use invertible transformations to map between data and latent space.
- **Autoregressive models:** Generate data sequentially, conditioning each output on previous outputs.
- **Normalizing flows:** Combine autoregressive models with invertible transformations.
- Generative models have the potential to revolutionize various fields by creating new and realistic data. They are used in creative applications, scientific research, and industrial tasks, providing valuable tools for data generation, exploration, and analysis.

FIVE

DEEP LEARNING FRAMEWORKS AND TOOLS

Popular Deep Learning Frameworks

Deep learning frameworks provide a high-level interface for building and training neural networks. They abstract away much of the underlying complexity, making it easier for developers to focus on the problem at hand. Here are some of the most popular deep learning frameworks:

TensorFlow

- **Developed by:** Google
- **Strengths:** Large community, extensive documentation, production-ready, supports a wide range of hardware accelerators (TPUs, GPUs).
- **Popular use cases:** Large-scale machine learning projects, research, production deployment.

PyTorch

- **Developed by:** Facebook AI Research

- **Strengths:** Dynamic computational graph, easy to use for prototyping, strong community, good integration with Python's scientific computing ecosystem.
- **Popular use cases:** Research, prototyping, natural language processing, computer vision.

Keras

- **High-level API:** Built on top of TensorFlow or Theano (now deprecated).
- **Strengths:** User-friendly interface, easy to learn, modular design, can be used with both TensorFlow and Theano backends.
- **Popular use cases:** Rapid prototyping, teaching deep learning concepts.

Other popular frameworks:

- **Caffe:** Developed by UC Berkeley, known for its speed and efficiency.
- **MXNet:** Developed by Apache Software Foundation, supports multiple programming languages.
- **CNTK:** Developed by Microsoft, designed for distributed training on large-scale datasets.

The choice of framework often depends on factors such as the specific task, team expertise, and desired level of flexibility. TensorFlow and PyTorch are generally considered the most popular and versatile options, while Keras is a good choice for beginners or those who prefer a simpler API.

It's also worth noting that many frameworks can be used together. For example, Keras can be used as a high-level API on top of TensorFlow or Theano. This allows developers to combine the best of both worlds, leveraging the flexibility of TensorFlow or Theano while benefiting from the simplicity of Keras.

Data Preparation and Preprocessing

Data preparation and preprocessing are crucial steps in the machine learning pipeline. They involve transforming raw data into a suitable format for training models and ensuring data quality.

Key tasks in data preparation and preprocessing:

Data collection: Data collection is a crucial step in the data science process that involves gathering relevant data from various sources. This can include databases, APIs, web scraping, sensors, social media platforms, and public datasets. Effective data collection requires careful planning and consideration of data quality, privacy, and ethical implications. By collecting high-quality and relevant data, data scientists can lay the foundation for valuable insights and analysis.

Data cleaning: Data cleaning is a critical step in the data science process that involves identifying and correcting errors, inconsistencies, and inaccuracies within a dataset. This process typically involves handling missing values, outliers, duplicates, and inconsistencies to ensure data quality and reliability. Missing values can be imputed using techniques like mean, median, or mode imputation, or by using more sophisticated methods like regression or machine learning. Outliers can be identified and removed or corrected based on statistical analysis or domain knowledge. Inconsistencies and duplicates can be detected and resolved through data validation and deduplication techniques. By effectively cleaning the data, data scientists can improve the accuracy and reliability of their analysis and models.

Data normalization: Data normalization is a common preprocessing step in data science that involves scaling numerical data to a specific range, typically between 0 and 1. This process helps to improve model convergence and prevent issues like numerical instability. Normalization techniques include min-max scaling, standardization, and normalization using a specific range. By normalizing data, features with different scales become comparable, allowing machine learning models to learn more effectively and avoid biases. Additionally, normalization can help to reduce the impact of outliers and improve the interpretability of model results.

Data transformation: Data transformation is a preprocessing step in data science that involves converting data into a suitable format for the machine learning model. This often involves transforming categorical variables into numerical representations, such as one-hot encoding or label encoding. Additionally, data transformation can include handling missing values, scaling numerical data, and creating new features through feature engineering. By transforming data into a compatible format, data scientists can ensure that the model can effectively learn from the data and make accurate predictions.

Feature engineering: Feature engineering is a critical step in the data science process that involves creating new features or transforming existing features to improve the performance of machine learning models. By carefully selecting and engineering relevant features, data scientists can extract more meaningful information from the data and enhance the model's ability to learn and make accurate predictions. Feature engineering techniques can include creating interaction terms, aggregating features, transforming categorical variables, and handling missing values. By investing time and effort into feature engineering, data scientists can significantly improve the performance and interpretability of their models.

Data splitting: Data splitting is a crucial step in the data science process that involves dividing the dataset into distinct training, validation, and testing sets. The training set is used to train the machine learning model, the validation set is used to tune hyperparameters and evaluate the model's performance during training, and the testing set is used to assess the model's final performance on unseen data. By carefully splitting the data, data scientists can ensure that the model is not overfitted to the training data and can generalize well to new data.

Common techniques for data preprocessing:

Imputation:

- **Handling Missing Values:** Imputation techniques are used to fill in missing values in the dataset. Common methods include using the mean, median, or mode of the column, or using machine learning algorithms to predict the missing values.

Outlier Detection:

- **Identifying Extreme Values:** Outlier detection techniques identify extreme values that can skew the data distribution. Common methods include statistical techniques like Z-score or IQR, or machine learning-based methods like isolation forests.

Normalization:

- **Scaling Data:** Normalization techniques scale numerical data to a specific range, such as between 0 and 1. This helps to prevent features with larger magnitudes from dominating the learning process. Common normalization techniques include min-max scaling, standardization, and normalization using a specific range.

One-Hot Encoding:

- **Converting Categorical Variables:** One-hot encoding converts categorical variables into numerical representations by creating a binary vector with one element set to 1 for the corresponding category and the rest set to 0.

Label Encoding:

- **Assigning Numerical Values:** Label encoding assigns numerical values to categorical variables, typically starting from 0. However, label encoding should be used with caution, as it assumes an ordinal relationship between the categories.

Feature Scaling:

- **Equalizing Feature Importance:** Feature scaling ensures that features with different magnitudes have an equal impact on the learning process. This prevents features with larger magnitudes from dominating the model.

Data Augmentation:

- **Increasing Dataset Size:** Data augmentation techniques create new data samples from existing ones to increase the dataset size and improve model generalization. This is particularly useful when the available dataset is small.

By effectively using these data preprocessing techniques, you can improve the quality and consistency of your data, making it more suitable for machine learning models.

Importance of data preparation and preprocessing:
Data Quality:

- **Accurate and Reliable Results:** Ensuring clean and accurate data is essential for obtaining reliable and accurate model results. Errors, inconsistencies, and missing values can introduce bias and noise into the data, leading to inaccurate predictions.

Model Performance:

- **Improved Accuracy:** Well-prepared data can significantly improve model accuracy and generalization. By addressing data quality issues and transforming data into a suitable format, you can help the model learn meaningful patterns and make accurate predictions.
- **Reduced Bias:** Proper data preparation can help to reduce bias in the data, leading to fairer and more equitable models.

Efficiency:

- **Faster Training:** Properly preprocessed data can reduce training time and computational resources. For example, normalizing data can improve convergence speed, and handling missing values can prevent errors during training.
- **Resource Optimization:** By optimizing data preparation, you can make the most efficient use of available computational resources.

Key Considerations:

- **Domain Knowledge:** Understanding the domain and the specific requirements of the task is essential for effective data preparation.
- **Iterative Process:** Data preparation is often an iterative process, and you may need to revisit and refine your approach as you gain more insights into the data and the model's performance.

By carefully preparing and preprocessing data, you can lay a strong foundation for building effective machine learning models that produce accurate and reliable results.

Model Training and Evaluation

Model training is the process of teaching a machine learning model to learn patterns and relationships from data. Model evaluation involves assessing the model's performance on unseen data to determine its effectiveness.

Model Training

1. **Choosing a suitable model architecture:** Select a model that is appropriate for the task and data type (e.g., neural network, decision tree, random forest).
2. **Preparing the training data:** Ensure the data is clean, preprocessed, and split into training and validation sets.

3. **Setting hyperparameters:** Choose appropriate hyperparameters for the model, such as learning rate, batch size, and number of epochs.
4. **Training the model:** Iterate through the training data multiple times (epochs), adjusting the model's parameters using backpropagation or other optimization algorithms.
5. **Monitoring the training process:** Track the model's performance on the training and validation sets to identify overfitting or underfitting.

Model Evaluation

1. **Using a holdout set:** Reserve a portion of the data as a testing set to evaluate the model's performance on unseen data.
2. **Calculating metrics:** Use appropriate metrics to measure the model's performance, depending on the task (e.g., accuracy, precision, recall, F1-score, mean squared error, mean absolute error).
3. **Interpreting results:** Analyze the evaluation metrics to assess the model's strengths and weaknesses.
4. **Iterating and refining:** If the model's performance is not satisfactory, experiment with different architectures, hyperparameters, or data preprocessing techniques.

Key considerations in model training and evaluation:
Overfitting:

- **Overly Complex Model:** Overfitting occurs when a model is too complex and learns the training data too well, including noise and outliers. This leads to poor performance on new, unseen data.
- **Symptoms:** High training accuracy but low validation/testing accuracy.

Underfitting:

- **Insufficient Complexity:** Underfitting occurs when a model is too simple and cannot capture the underlying patterns in the data. This leads to poor performance on both training and validation/testing data.
- **Symptoms:** Low training and validation/testing accuracy.

Bias and Variance:

- **Bias:** Bias refers to the model's systematic error. A high-bias model is underfitted and cannot capture the underlying patterns in the data.
- **Variance:** Variance refers to the model's sensitivity to different training sets. A high-variance model is overfitted and performs poorly on new data.
- **Bias-Variance Trade-off:** The goal is to find a balance between bias and variance to achieve optimal model performance.

Regularization:

- **Preventing Overfitting:** Regularization techniques, such as L1 and L2 regularization, dropout, and early stopping, can help to prevent overfitting by penalizing complex models and encouraging generalization.

By understanding these concepts and addressing overfitting, underfitting, bias, and variance, you can build more accurate and reliable machine learning models. By following these steps and considering the key factors, you can effectively train and evaluate machine learning models to achieve optimal performance on your specific tasks.

SIX
OVERFITTING AND UNDERFITTING

Understanding Overfitting and Underfitting

Overfitting and underfitting are two common challenges in machine learning. They occur when a model is either too complex or too simple to accurately represent the underlying patterns in the data.

Overfitting
Definition:

- **Overly Complex Model:** Overfitting occurs when a model is too complex and learns the training data too well, including noise and outliers. This means the model memorizes the training data instead of learning general patterns that can be applied to new data.

Consequences:

- **Poor Generalization:** Overfitting leads to poor performance on new, unseen data. The model may be unable to generalize its knowledge to new examples, resulting in high error rates.

Symptoms:

- **High Training Accuracy**: Overfitted models often exhibit high accuracy on the training set but perform poorly on the validation or testing set.
- **Low Validation/Testing Accuracy**: The discrepancy between high training accuracy and low validation/testing accuracy is a strong indicator of overfitting.

Causes:

- **Excessive Model Complexity**: Using a model that is too complex for the given task can increase the risk of overfitting.
- **Insufficient Training Data**: If the training dataset is too small or not representative of the real-world data, the model may overfit to the limited data.
- **Lack of Regularization**: Overfitting can be exacerbated by a lack of regularization techniques, which help to prevent the model from becoming too complex.

Addressing Overfitting:

- **Reduce Model Complexity**: Simplify the model by reducing the number of layers, neurons, or features.
- **Increase Training Data**: Collect more data to provide the model with a larger and more diverse dataset.
- **Regularization Techniques**: Use regularization techniques like L1/L2 regularization or dropout to penalize model complexity and prevent overfitting.

By understanding the concept of overfitting and taking steps to address it, you can build more robust and reliable machine learning models.

Underfitting

Definition:

- **Insufficient Complexity:** Underfitting occurs when a model is too simple and cannot capture the underlying patterns in the data. This means the model is unable to learn the complex relationships between the features and the target variable.

Consequences:

- **Poor Performance:** Underfitting leads to poor performance on both training and validation/testing data. The model is unable to generalize its knowledge to new data, resulting in high error rates.

Symptoms:

- **Low Training and Validation/Testing Accuracy:** Both training and validation/testing accuracy are low, indicating that the model is unable to learn the underlying patterns in the data.

Causes:

- **Insufficient Model Complexity:** Using a model that is too simple for the given task can lead to underfitting. A more complex model may be needed to capture the underlying patterns.
- **Insufficient Training Data:** If the training dataset is too small or not representative of the real-world data, the model may be unable to learn the underlying patterns.
- **Inappropriate Feature Engineering:** If the features used to train the model are not relevant or informative, the model may struggle to capture the underlying patterns.

Addressing Underfitting:

- **Increase Model Complexity:** Add more layers, neurons, or features to the model to increase its complexity.

- **Increase Training Data:** Collect more data to provide the model with a larger and more diverse dataset.
- **Improve Feature Engineering:** Carefully select and engineer relevant features to ensure that the model can learn meaningful patterns.

By understanding the concept of underfitting and taking steps to address it, you can build more robust and accurate machine learning models.

Identifying Overfitting and Underfitting

Learning Curves:

- **Visualizing Performance:** Learning curves plot the training and validation loss over time. If the validation loss starts to increase while the training loss continues to decrease, it's a strong indicator of overfitting. This means the model is learning the training data too well but struggling to generalize to new data.

Cross-Validation:

- **Evaluating Generalization:** Cross-validation involves dividing the data into multiple folds and training the model on different subsets to assess its generalization performance. This helps to identify overfitting by evaluating the model's performance on unseen data.
- **Common Techniques:** Common cross-validation techniques include k-fold cross-validation and stratified k-fold cross-validation.

Regularization Techniques:

- **Preventing Overfitting:** Regularization techniques like L1 and L2 regularization can help to prevent overfitting by penalizing complex models. These techniques encourage the model to have simpler weights, making it less likely to overfit the training data.

Additional Techniques:

- **Early Stopping:** Early stopping involves stopping training when the validation loss starts to increase, even if the training loss is still decreasing. This can help to prevent overfitting by stopping the training process before the model starts to memorize the training data.
- **Feature Engineering:** Careful feature engineering can help to improve model performance and reduce the risk of overfitting. By selecting relevant features and transforming them appropriately, you can provide the model with meaningful information and avoid overfitting.

By using these techniques, you can effectively identify and address overfitting and underfitting in your machine learning models, leading to improved performance and generalization.

Addressing Overfitting and Underfitting
Gather More Data:

- **Data Diversity:** Increasing the amount and diversity of training data can help to reduce overfitting by providing the model with more examples to learn from. This can help the model generalize better to new data.

Simplify the Model:

- **Reduce Complexity:** If a model is too complex, simplifying it by reducing the number of layers, neurons, or features can help to prevent overfitting. This can make the model less prone to memorizing the training data and more likely to generalize well.

Regularization:

- **Penalty Term:** Regularization techniques, such as L1 and L2 regularization, add a penalty term to the loss function that discourages complex models. This helps to prevent overfitting by encouraging the model to have simpler weights.

Feature Engineering:

- **Relevant Features:** Creating more relevant features can improve model performance and reduce the risk of overfitting. By selecting features that are informative and relevant to the task, you can provide the model with the necessary information to learn meaningful patterns.

Early Stopping:

- **Monitor Validation Loss:** Early stopping involves monitoring the validation loss during training and stopping the training process when the validation loss starts to increase. This helps to prevent overfitting by stopping the training before the model starts to memorize the training data.

By understanding and addressing overfitting and underfitting, you can build more accurate and reliable machine learning models. These strategies can be used in combination to find the optimal balance between model complexity and data fit.

Regularization Techniques

Regularization techniques are used to prevent overfitting in machine learning models. They introduce a penalty term to the loss function, discouraging the model from becoming too complex and learning noise in the data.

L1 Regularization (Lasso Regression)

L1 regularization, also known as Lasso regression, is a regularization technique that adds a penalty term to the loss function. This penalty term is the absolute value of the weights, which encourages the model to learn sparse solutions.

Here's a more detailed explanation:

- **Penalty term:** The L1 regularization penalty term is calculated as the sum of the absolute values of the weights:
- L1_penalty = sum(|w_i|)

where w_i are the model's weights.

- **Effect:** By adding this penalty term to the loss function, L1 regularization encourages the model to drive some weights to zero. This effectively selects the most important features and reduces the complexity of the model.
- **Usefulness:** L1 regularization is particularly useful for sparse models, where only a subset of features is important. It can help to prevent overfitting and improve the model's generalization performance.

In summary, L1 regularization is a valuable technique for feature selection and building sparse models. It can be used in various machine learning tasks, such as regression, classification, and dimensionality reduction.

L2 Regularization (Ridge Regression)

L2 regularization, also known as Ridge regression, is another regularization technique that adds a penalty term to the loss function. However, unlike L1 regularization, the L2 penalty term is the squared sum of the weights.

Here's a more detailed explanation:

- **Penalty term:** The L2 regularization penalty term is calculated as the sum of the squared weights:
- L2_penalty = sum(w_i^2)

where w_i are the model's weights.

- **Effect:** By adding this penalty term to the loss function, L2 regularization encourages the model to shrink the weights towards zero but doesn't force them to become exactly zero. This helps to prevent overfitting by reducing the model's complexity.

- **Usefulness**: L2 regularization is generally useful for preventing overfitting in machine learning models, especially when multiple features are important. It can help to improve the model's generalization performance and make it more robust to noise in the data.

In summary, L2 regularization is a valuable technique for preventing overfitting and improving the performance of machine learning models. It is often used in conjunction with other regularization techniques, such as L1 regularization, to achieve the desired level of regularization.

Dropout
Technique:

- **Random Dropout**: Dropout involves randomly dropping out neurons during training with a certain probability. This means that some neurons are deactivated during each training iteration, forcing the model to learn more robust representations.

Effect:

- **Introduces Noise**: Dropout introduces noise into the training process, preventing the model from relying too heavily on any particular neuron or group of neurons. This makes the model more robust to changes in the input data.
- **Prevents Co-adaptation**: By randomly dropping out neurons, dropout prevents co-adaptation between neurons, which can occur when neurons become too dependent on each other.

Useful for:

- **Preventing Overfitting**: Dropout is a highly effective technique for preventing overfitting in deep neural networks, especially for large models with many layers and neurons.

- **Improving Generalization:** By making the model more robust to noise and preventing co-adaptation, dropout can help to improve the model's generalization performance.

In summary, dropout is a valuable regularization technique that can significantly improve the performance of deep neural networks. By introducing noise and preventing co-adaptation, dropout helps to reduce overfitting and improve the model's ability to generalize to new data.

Other Regularization Techniques
Early Stopping:

- **Monitor Validation Loss:** Early stopping involves monitoring the validation loss during training and stopping the training process when the validation loss starts to increase. This helps to prevent overfitting by stopping the training before the model starts to memorize the training data.
- **Prevent Overfitting:** By stopping training early, you can avoid overfitting the model to the training data and improve its generalization performance.

Data Augmentation:

- **Increase Dataset Size:** Data augmentation involves creating new training examples from existing data to increase the size and diversity of the dataset. This can help to improve the model's generalization performance by exposing it to a wider range of examples.
- **Common Techniques:** Common data augmentation techniques include random rotations, translations, scaling, and flipping.

Batch Normalization:

- **Normalize Inputs:** Batch normalization normalizes the inputs to each layer of a neural network. This helps to improve training stability and reduce the need for careful initialization of the model's parameters.
- **Accelerate Training:** Batch normalization can also accelerate the training process, making it possible to train deeper and more complex models.

By using these techniques, you can improve the performance of your deep learning models and make them more robust to overfitting and other challenges. Choosing the right regularization technique depends on the specific task and model architecture. Experimentation is often necessary to find the best approach. In some cases, combining multiple regularization techniques can be effective. By using regularization techniques, you can build more robust and generalizable machine learning models that are less likely to overfit the training data.

Hyperparameter Tuning

Hyperparameters are parameters that are set before training a machine learning model. They control the behavior of the model and can significantly impact its performance. Hyperparameter tuning involves systematically searching for the optimal combination of hyperparameters to maximize model performance.

Common hyperparameters:

Learning Rate:

- **Step Size:** The learning rate controls the step size during gradient descent, which is the optimization algorithm used to update the model's parameters.
- **Impact:** A higher learning rate can lead to faster convergence but may also result in instability. A lower learning rate can be more stable but may take longer to converge.

Batch Size:

- **Number of Samples:** The batch size determines the number of samples processed in each iteration of training.
- **Impact:** Larger batch sizes can lead to faster training but may require more memory. Smaller batch sizes can be more noisy and may require more iterations to converge.

Number of Epochs:

- **Training Iterations:** The number of epochs determines how many times the entire dataset is passed through the model during training.
- **Impact:** More epochs can improve model performance but may also lead to overfitting.

Hidden Layer Size:

- **Model Capacity:** The hidden layer size determines the capacity of the neural network. Larger hidden layers can improve model performance but may also increase the risk of overfitting.

Activation Function:

- **Non-Linearity:** Activation functions introduce non-linearity into neural networks, allowing them to learn complex patterns. Common activation functions include ReLU, sigmoid, and tanh.

Regularization Strength:

- **Preventing Overfitting:** Regularization techniques, such as L1 and L2 regularization, add a penalty term to the loss function to prevent overfitting. The regularization strength controls the severity of the penalty.

Optimizer:

- **Parameter Updates:** The optimizer is the algorithm used to update the model's parameters during training. Common optimizers include SGD (Stochastic Gradient Descent), Adam, and RMSprop.

By carefully tuning these hyperparameters, you can significantly improve the performance of your machine learning models.

Hyperparameter tuning techniques:

Grid Search:

- **Exhaustive Search:** Grid search involves defining a grid of hyperparameter values and exhaustively trying all possible combinations.
- **Time-Consuming:** Grid search can be computationally expensive, especially for large search spaces.

Random Search:

- **Random Sampling:** Random search randomly samples hyperparameter values from a specified distribution.
- **Efficiency:** Random search is often more efficient than grid search, especially for large search spaces.

Bayesian Optimization:

- **Probabilistic Modeling:** Bayesian optimization uses probabilistic models to efficiently explore the hyperparameter space. It learns from past evaluations to make informed decisions about which hyperparameter combinations to try next.
- **Efficiency:** Bayesian optimization can be more efficient than grid search and random search, especially for complex search spaces.

Gradient-Based Optimization:

- **Gradient Information:** Gradient-based optimization uses gradient information to update hyperparameters iteratively. This allows for more efficient exploration of the search space.
- **Challenges:** Gradient-based optimization can be challenging to apply to hyperparameter tuning, as hyperparameters are typically discrete values. However, techniques like gradient-based meta-learning can be used to address this challenge.

By understanding these hyperparameter tuning techniques, you can choose the most appropriate method for your specific machine learning task and computational resources.

Considerations in hyperparameter tuning:

Computational Cost:

- **Resource Requirements:** Hyperparameter tuning can be computationally expensive, especially for large models and datasets. It may require significant computational resources, such as powerful GPUs or TPUs.
- **Time Constraints:** The computational cost of hyperparameter tuning can be a limiting factor, especially for time-sensitive applications.

Overfitting:

- **Validation Set:** It's important to be cautious of overfitting the hyperparameters to the validation set. This can lead to a model that performs well on the validation set but poorly on unseen data.
- **Nested Cross-Validation:** Nested cross-validation can help to address this issue by using an inner loop for hyperparameter tuning and an outer loop for evaluating the final model performance.

Time Constraints:

- **Task Importance:** The time available for hyperparameter tuning should be considered in relation to the importance of the task. For critical applications, it may be worth investing more time and computational resources into hyperparameter tuning.
- **Trade-offs:** There may be trade-offs between the time spent on hyperparameter tuning and the final model performance. It's important to balance these factors based on the specific requirements of the task.

By carefully considering these factors, you can effectively tune hyperparameters while balancing computational cost, overfitting, and time constraints.

Tools and libraries for hyperparameter tuning:

The various tools available for hyperparameter optimization. Let's break down each tool in more detail:

Scikit-learn:

- **Grid Search:** This is a brute-force approach where the algorithm tries all possible combinations of hyperparameters within a specified grid. It's simple to implement but can be computationally expensive for large search spaces.
- **Random Search:** A more efficient approach that randomly samples hyperparameter combinations from the search space. It often performs better than grid search, especially for large search spaces.

Hyperopt:

- **Bayesian Optimization:** This probabilistic approach uses Bayesian statistics to model the relationship between hyperparameters and the objective function. It learns from past evaluations to make more informed decisions about which hyperparameter combinations to try next.

Optuna:

- **Tree-structured Parzen Estimator (TPE):** Optuna primarily uses TPE for hyperparameter optimization. TPE is a Bayesian optimization algorithm that is designed to be efficient and scalable.

Ray Tune:

- **Scalable Hyperparameter Tuning:** Ray Tune is a distributed hyperparameter tuning framework that can be used to scale hyperparameter optimization experiments across multiple machines. It provides features like early stopping, asynchronous hyperparameter tuning, and integration with other Ray components.

Each tool has its own strengths and weaknesses, and the best choice depends on factors such as the size of the search space, computational resources, and the desired level of efficiency. Effective hyperparameter tuning is essential for maximizing the performance of machine learning models. By carefully selecting and optimizing hyperparameters, you can improve model accuracy, generalization, and efficiency.

SEVEN
ETHICAL CONSIDERATIONS IN DEEP LEARNING

Bias and Fairness in AI

Bias and fairness are critical concerns in the development and deployment of artificial intelligence (AI) systems. Bias occurs when an AI system exhibits unfair or discriminatory behavior, often reflecting the biases present in the data it is trained on. Fairness, on the other hand, refers to the equitable treatment of different groups or individuals by an AI system.

Sources of bias in AI:

Biased data: Biased data can have a significant impact on the performance and fairness of AI models. Here's a more detailed explanation:

- **Perpetuating Bias:** When an AI model is trained on biased data, it can learn and perpetuate the biases present in the data. This can lead to unfair or discriminatory outcomes.
- **Examples of Bias:** Bias in data can occur due to various factors, such as sampling bias, measurement bias, or historical biases. For example, if a dataset used to train a facial recognition system

primarily includes images of white people, the model may struggle to accurately recognize people of color.

To address bias in AI systems, it's essential to use diverse and representative datasets, develop techniques to detect and mitigate bias, and ensure that AI systems are evaluated for fairness. By taking these steps, we can help to create AI systems that are unbiased and equitable.

Algorithmic bias: The algorithms themselves can be biased, either due to design flaws or unintended consequences.

- **Social bias:** Human biases can be inadvertently introduced into AI systems during development or deployment.

Consequences of bias in AI:

- **Discrimination:** Biased AI systems can discriminate against certain groups, leading to unfair outcomes.
- **Lack of trust:** Bias can erode public trust in AI and hinder its adoption.
- **Ethical concerns:** Biased AI systems raise ethical questions about fairness, accountability, and transparency.

Addressing bias and promoting fairness in AI:
Diverse Datasets:

- **Representation:** Ensure that the data used to train AI models is diverse and representative of the population it will serve. This helps to avoid biases that may be present in the data.
- **Avoiding Bias:** By using diverse datasets, AI models can be trained to recognize and avoid biases that may be present in the data.

Fairness Metrics:

- **Measurement and Evaluation:** Develop and use metrics to measure and evaluate fairness in AI systems. These metrics can help to identify and address biases.
- **Examples of Fairness Metrics:** Examples of fairness metrics include demographic parity, equal opportunity, and predictive parity.

Bias Detection and Mitigation:

- **Identifying Sources of Bias:** Identify sources of bias in AI systems, such as biases in the data, algorithms, or decision-making processes.
- **Mitigation Techniques:** Use techniques like adversarial training, re-weighting, and fair classification to mitigate biases.

Transparency and Explainability:

- **Understanding Decision-Making:** Make AI systems more transparent and explainable to increase accountability. This involves developing techniques to understand how AI systems make decisions and identify potential biases.
- **Building Trust:** Transparency and explainability can help to build trust in AI systems and ensure that they are used responsibly.

Ethical Guidelines:

- **Developing and Following Guidelines:** Develop and follow ethical guidelines for AI development and deployment that prioritize fairness and equity. These guidelines should address issues such as bias, discrimination, and accountability.
- **Responsible Use:** Ensuring that AI systems are used responsibly and ethically is crucial for avoiding harmful consequences and promoting fairness.

By implementing these strategies, organizations can help to ensure that AI systems are fair, equitable, and avoid perpetuating biases. It is essential to address bias and promote fairness in AI to ensure that these systems are used responsibly and benefit society as a whole. By understanding the sources of bias and taking proactive steps to mitigate it, we can create AI systems that are equitable, trustworthy, and aligned with our values.

Privacy and Data Security in AI

Privacy and data security are critical concerns in the development and deployment of AI systems. As AI systems increasingly rely on large amounts of personal data, it is essential to protect individuals' privacy and ensure the security of their data.

Privacy concerns in AI:

- **Data collection and usage:** The collection and use of personal data for AI purposes can raise privacy concerns, especially when data is collected without individuals' knowledge or consent.
- **Data sharing:** Sharing data with third parties can expose it to additional risks and privacy breaches.
- **Algorithmic accountability:** It can be difficult to understand how AI algorithms make decisions, which can raise questions about transparency and accountability.

Data security risks in AI:

- **Data breaches:** Unauthorized access to or theft of personal data can have serious consequences.
- **Malicious use:** AI systems can be misused for malicious purposes, such as identity theft or fraud.
- **Data poisoning:** Attackers can manipulate training data to compromise the accuracy and fairness of AI models.

Addressing privacy and data security concerns in AI:
Data Minimization:

- **Collect Only Necessary Data:** Only collect the data that is absolutely necessary to achieve the desired outcome. Avoid collecting unnecessary personal information.

Consent:

- **Informed Consent:** Obtain informed consent from individuals before collecting and using their data. This means providing clear information about how the data will be used and obtaining explicit consent from the individual.

Data Anonymization and Pseudonymization:

- **Remove Identifiers:** Anonymize data by removing personally identifiable information (PII) such as names, addresses, and email addresses.
- **Pseudonymize Data:** Pseudonymize data by replacing PII with pseudonyms or codes, making it difficult to link the data back to specific individuals.

Data Encryption:

- **Protect Data in Transit and at Rest:** Use encryption techniques to protect data both in transit (while being transmitted) and at rest (when stored). This prevents unauthorized access and interception of data.

Access Controls:

- **Limit Access:** Implement strong access controls to limit access to sensitive data to authorized personnel only. This includes using role-based access control (RBAC) and implementing strong authentication and authorization mechanisms.

Regular Monitoring and Auditing:

- **Identify Vulnerabilities:** Regularly monitor AI systems for security vulnerabilities and privacy breaches. Conduct security audits to identify and address potential risks.
- **Proactive Measures:** Implement proactive measures to prevent security breaches, such as intrusion detection systems and regular vulnerability assessments.

Ethical Guidelines:

- **Develop and Follow Guidelines:** Develop and follow ethical guidelines for AI development and deployment that prioritize privacy and security. These guidelines should address issues such as data collection, use, sharing, and protection.

By implementing these strategies, organizations can significantly enhance the privacy and security of their AI systems and build trust with users. By addressing privacy and data security concerns, we can ensure that AI systems are developed and used in a responsible and ethical manner. It is essential to strike a balance between the benefits of AI and the protection of individuals' privacy and rights.

Responsible AI Development

Responsible AI development involves considering the ethical, social, and environmental implications of AI systems. It ensures that AI is developed and deployed in a way that benefits society and minimizes harm.

Key principles of responsible AI development:
Beneficial:

- **Positive Impact:** AI should be developed to improve people's lives and address societal challenges. This includes applications in healthcare, education, climate change, and other areas where AI can have a positive impact.
- **Avoiding Harm:** It's important to ensure that AI systems are not used to harm individuals or groups. This includes avoiding

applications that could lead to discrimination, surveillance, or other negative consequences.

Fair:

- **Bias Mitigation:** AI systems should be developed to avoid perpetuating biases that exist in society. This includes addressing biases in data, algorithms, and decision-making processes.
- **Equal Treatment:** AI systems should treat all individuals fairly and avoid discrimination based on factors such as race, gender, age, or socioeconomic status.

Transparent:

- **Explainability:** AI systems should be designed to be transparent and explainable, allowing users to understand how they make decisions. This can help to build trust and accountability.
- **Bias Detection:** Transparent AI systems can also help to identify and mitigate biases.

Accountable:

- **Responsibility:** Developers and organizations should be held accountable for the actions of their AI systems. This includes ensuring that the systems are used responsibly and ethically.
- **Legal and Ethical Frameworks:** Clear legal and ethical frameworks should be established to govern the development and deployment of AI systems.

Ethical:

- **Human Values:** AI development should align with human values and avoid harmful consequences. This includes considering the potential negative impacts of AI and taking steps to mitigate

them.
- **Ethical Guidelines:** Ethical guidelines and principles should be established to guide AI development and ensure that it is conducted responsibly.

By adhering to these principles, we can help ensure that AI is developed and used in a way that benefits society and avoids harmful consequences.

Areas of focus for responsible AI development:
Bias and Fairness:

- **Identifying and Mitigating Bias:** Identifying and addressing biases in AI systems is crucial to ensure equitable treatment of different groups. This involves collecting diverse data, using unbiased algorithms, and developing fairness metrics.
- **Avoiding Discrimination:** AI systems should not be used to discriminate against individuals based on factors such as race, gender, age, or socioeconomic status.

Privacy and Data Security:

- **Data Protection:** Protecting individuals' privacy and ensuring the security of data used in AI systems is essential. This includes implementing strong data protection measures, obtaining informed consent, and adhering to relevant privacy regulations.
- **Data Privacy Laws:** Compliance with data privacy laws, such as the General Data Protection Regulation (GDPR) and the California Consumer Privacy Act (CCPA), is essential for organizations that handle personal data.

Explainability:

- **Understanding Decision-Making:** Making AI systems more transparent and understandable can help to build trust and accountability. This involves developing techniques to explain how AI systems make decisions and identify potential biases.

- **Transparency and Accountability:** Transparency and accountability are essential for ensuring that AI systems are used responsibly and ethically.

Human Oversight:

- **Human Control:** Ensuring that humans have oversight and control over AI systems is crucial to prevent unintended consequences. This involves developing guidelines and procedures for human intervention and oversight.
- **Preventing Harm:** Human oversight can help to identify and prevent harmful outcomes that may arise from AI systems.

Environmental Impact:

- **Energy Consumption:** The development and deployment of AI systems can have a significant environmental impact, particularly in terms of energy consumption.
- **Sustainable Practices:** It's important to consider the environmental impact of AI and develop sustainable practices to minimize its negative effects.

By addressing these areas, we can help ensure that AI is developed and used responsibly and ethically, benefiting society while minimizing risks.

Challenges and opportunities in responsible AI development: Technical Challenges:

- **Bias Detection and Mitigation:** Developing techniques to identify and mitigate biases in AI systems can be technically challenging.
- **Explainability:** Making AI systems more transparent and understandable requires developing new methods and techniques.

- **Scalability:** Ensuring that AI systems can be scaled to handle large and complex datasets while maintaining performance and efficiency can be technically challenging.

Ethical Challenges:

- **Balancing Benefits and Risks:** Balancing the potential benefits of AI with the risks and ethical concerns is a complex task.
- **Avoiding Harm:** Ensuring that AI systems are not used to harm individuals or groups requires careful consideration and ethical guidelines.

Regulatory Challenges:

- **Developing Regulations:** Creating comprehensive and effective regulations for AI development is a complex and ongoing process.
- **Global Coordination:** Developing global standards and regulations for AI can be challenging due to differences in cultural, legal, and political contexts.

Collaboration:

- **Multidisciplinary Approach:** Addressing the challenges of responsible AI requires collaboration between researchers, policymakers, industry leaders, and other stakeholders.
- **Shared Goals:** Fostering a shared vision and understanding of the importance of responsible AI development is essential for driving progress.

Future Outlook:

By addressing these challenges and following the principles of responsible AI development, we can create AI systems that benefit society and avoid harmful consequences. This will require ongoing research, collaboration, and a commitment to ethical and responsible AI development.

Responsible AI development is essential for ensuring that AI is used for good and avoids harmful consequences. By following these principles and addressing the challenges, we can create AI systems that benefit society and contribute to a more equitable and sustainable future.

EIGHT
FUTURE TRENDS AND CHALLENGES

Emerging Deep Learning Techniques

Deep learning is a rapidly evolving field, with new techniques emerging constantly. Here are some of the most promising emerging techniques:

Transformers

Transformers have become a powerful and versatile architecture in the field of natural language processing (NLP) and beyond.

Here's a more detailed explanation of transformers and their key components:

Attention Mechanism:

- **Focus on Relevant Parts:** The attention mechanism allows the model to focus on different parts of the input data at different times. This is especially useful in tasks like machine translation, where the model needs to consider the entire source sentence to generate the target sentence.
- **Weighted Sum:** The attention mechanism calculates a weighted sum of the input sequence, where the weights represent the importance of each element in relation to the current output.

Self-Attention:

- **Relating Different Parts:** Self-attention enables the model to relate different parts of the input sequence to each other, capturing long-range dependencies. For example, in a sentence, self-attention can help the model understand the relationship between a pronoun and its antecedent.
- **Contextual Understanding:** Self-attention allows the model to understand the context of each word in the sequence, making it more effective for tasks that require understanding the overall meaning of the text.

Applications:

- **Natural Language Processing:** Transformers have achieved state-of-the-art results on a wide range of NLP tasks, including machine translation, text summarization, question answering, and text generation.
- **Machine Translation:** Transformers have significantly improved the quality of machine translation systems, especially for long and complex sentences.
- **Text Summarization:** Transformers can generate concise and informative summaries of long documents.
- **Image Generation:** Transformers have also been applied to image generation tasks, where they can generate high-quality images based on text descriptions.

In summary, transformers are a powerful architecture that has revolutionized the field of natural language processing and is being applied to a variety of other tasks as well. Their ability to capture long-range dependencies and focus on relevant parts of the input data makes them well-suited for tasks that require understanding the context and relationships between different elements in a sequence.

Graph Neural Networks (GNNs)

Graph Neural Networks (GNNs) are a powerful class of neural networks specifically designed to process data represented as graphs.

Here's a more detailed explanation:

Graph-Structured Data:

- **Nodes and Edges:** Graphs are composed of nodes (vertices) and edges (connections) that represent the relationships between nodes. This structure is ideal for representing data where the relationships between entities are important, such as social networks, molecular structures, and knowledge graphs.
- **Applications:** GNNs have found applications in various domains, including drug discovery, recommendation systems, social network analysis, and traffic prediction.

Message Passing:

- **Information Propagation:** GNNs use a message passing mechanism to propagate information between nodes in the graph. This allows the nodes to learn representations that capture the structural properties and context of the graph.
- **Aggregation and Update:** In each iteration, nodes aggregate information from their neighbors and update their own representations. This process is repeated multiple times, allowing the GNN to learn complex patterns and relationships within the graph.

Applications:

- **Drug Discovery:** GNNs can be used to predict the properties of molecules and identify potential drug candidates.
- **Recommendation Systems:** GNNs can capture the complex relationships between users and items in recommendation systems, leading to more accurate and personalized recommendations.
- **Social Network Analysis:** GNNs can analyze social networks to identify communities, detect anomalies, and understand the

spread of information.

- **Traffic Prediction:** GNNs can be used to model traffic patterns in road networks and predict traffic congestion.

In summary, GNNs are a valuable tool for processing graph-structured data and have found applications in a wide range of domains. Their ability to capture the structural properties and relationships within graphs makes them well-suited for tasks that involve complex interconnected data.

Generative Adversarial Networks (GANs) with StyleGAN

Generative Adversarial Networks (GANs) and their variant, StyleGAN, have made significant advancements in image generation.

Here's a more detailed explanation:

Generative Adversarial Networks (GANs):

- **Generator and Discriminator:** GANs consist of two neural networks: a generator and a discriminator. The generator creates new images, while the discriminator tries to distinguish between real and generated images.
- **Adversarial Training:** The generator and discriminator are trained in an adversarial process, where they compete against each other. The generator aims to create images that are indistinguishable from real images, while the discriminator aims to accurately identify real and fake images.

StyleGAN:

- **Improved Image Quality:** StyleGAN is a more advanced architecture that generates high-quality, diverse images compared to earlier GANs. It introduces a style-based architecture that allows for fine-grained control over the generated images.
- **Applications:** StyleGAN has a wide range of applications, including:

- ○ **Image Generation:** Creating realistic images of people, animals, objects, and scenes.
- ○ **Art Creation:** Generating artistic styles and creating new art forms.
- ○ **Data Augmentation:** Increasing the size and diversity of datasets for training machine learning models.

In summary, GANs and StyleGAN have revolutionized image generation, enabling the creation of highly realistic and diverse images. These models have found applications in various fields, from art and design to scientific research.

Neural Architecture Search (NAS)

Neural Architecture Search (NAS) is a powerful technique for automatically designing neural network architectures.

Here's a more detailed explanation:

Automated Architecture Design:

- **Search Space:** NAS algorithms explore a vast search space of possible neural network architectures, considering different combinations of layers, hyperparameters, and operations.
- **Optimization:** The goal of NAS is to find the optimal architecture that achieves the best performance on a given task. This is typically done by using reinforcement learning, evolutionary algorithms, or gradient-based optimization.

Efficiency:

- **Computational Efficiency:** NAS can discover architectures that are more computationally efficient than manually designed ones. This is especially important for applications with limited computational resources or real-time constraints.
- **Performance Optimization:** NAS can also help to find architectures that achieve better performance on a given task, such as higher accuracy or lower error rates.

Applications:

- **Image Classification:** NAS has been used to design efficient and accurate architectures for image classification tasks.
- **Natural Language Processing:** NAS can be used to discover optimal architectures for tasks such as machine translation, text summarization, and question answering.
- **Computer Vision:** NAS can be used to design architectures for tasks like object detection, image segmentation, and image generation.

In summary, NAS is a valuable tool for automating the design of neural network architectures. By exploring a vast search space and optimizing for performance and efficiency, NAS can help to discover innovative and effective architectures for various machine learning tasks.

Reinforcement Learning with Deep Neural Networks

Reinforcement learning with deep neural networks is a powerful approach to solving complex decision-making problems.

Here's a more detailed explanation:

Decision-making Tasks:

- **Agent-Environment Interaction:** Reinforcement learning involves an agent interacting with an environment. The agent's goal is to learn a policy that maximizes a reward signal.
- **Deep Neural Networks:** By combining reinforcement learning with deep neural networks, the agent can learn complex representations of the environment and make informed decisions.

Applications:

- **Robotics:** Reinforcement learning with deep neural networks has been used to train robots to perform tasks such as grasping objects, navigating environments, and interacting with humans.

- **Game Playing:** Deep neural networks have been used to create AI agents that can play games at a superhuman level, such as Go and StarCraft II.
- **Autonomous Systems:** Reinforcement learning can be used to train autonomous systems, such as self-driving cars, to make decisions in complex and dynamic environments.

Key Concepts:

- **State:** The current situation of the agent in the environment. This can be represented as a set of variables that describe the agent's position, velocity, and other relevant information.
- **Action:** The choices available to the agent. The agent's actions can be discrete (e.g., move left, move right) or continuous (e.g., change velocity).
- **Reward:** A signal that indicates the success or failure of an action. The reward function defines the goal of the agent and provides feedback on its actions.
- **Policy:** A function that maps states to actions. The policy determines the agent's behavior and is learned through interaction with the environment.
- **Value Function:** A function that estimates the expected future reward from a given state. The value function helps the agent to make decisions that maximize long-term rewards.

By combining reinforcement learning with deep neural networks, agents can learn to make complex decisions in challenging environments. This approach has led to significant advancements in robotics, game playing, and autonomous systems.

Federated Learning

Federated learning is a powerful technique for training machine learning models on decentralized data while preserving privacy and security.

Here's a more detailed explanation:

Distributed Training:

- **Multiple Devices:** In federated learning, models are trained on multiple devices, such as smartphones, laptops, or IoT devices.
- **Local Updates:** Each device trains a local model using its own data.
- **Central Server:** The local models are periodically sent to a central server, where they are aggregated to create a global model.

Privacy and Security:

- **Data Privacy:** Federated learning avoids the need to share raw data with a central server, preserving user privacy.
- **Security:** The decentralized nature of federated learning makes it more resilient to attacks on the central server.

Applications:

- **Medical Imaging:** Federated learning can be used to train medical imaging models on data from multiple hospitals, while preserving patient privacy.
- **Mobile Apps:** Mobile apps can use federated learning to improve their performance and personalization without compromising user privacy.
- **IoT Devices:** Federated learning can be used to train models on data from IoT devices, such as smart home devices or sensors, while maintaining data security.

In summary, federated learning is a promising technique for training machine learning models on decentralized data while preserving privacy and security. It has a wide range of applications, from medical imaging to mobile apps and IoT devices. These are just a few examples of emerging deep learning techniques. The field is constantly evolving, and new techniques are being developed to address specific challenges and improve performance in various domains.

Challenges and Limitations of Deep Learning

Despite its impressive achievements, deep learning is not without its challenges and limitations. Here are some of the key issues:

Data Requirements

Data requirements are crucial for successful deep learning applications. Here's a more detailed explanation of the key factors:

Large Datasets:

- **Training and Validation:** Deep learning models typically require large amounts of high-quality data to train effectively. This data is used to teach the model patterns and relationships, enabling it to make accurate predictions.
- **Diversity:** The data should be diverse to represent the real-world scenarios the model will encounter.

Data Scarcity:

- **Challenges:** In some domains, obtaining sufficient data can be challenging or expensive. This is particularly true for specialized or emerging fields where data may be limited.
- **Data Augmentation:** Techniques like data augmentation can help to increase the size and diversity of datasets, but they may not always be sufficient.

Data Quality:

- **Impact on Performance:** The quality of the data significantly impacts model performance. Noise, errors, and inconsistencies in the data can lead to inaccurate results.
- **Data Cleaning and Preprocessing:** Data cleaning and preprocessing are essential steps to ensure data quality and improve model performance.

In summary, access to large, high-quality datasets is crucial for training effective deep learning models. Addressing data scarcity and ensuring data quality are critical challenges that need to be carefully considered in deep learning projects.

Computational Resources

Computational resources are a significant factor to consider when working with deep learning models. Here's a more detailed explanation:

Hardware Demands:

- **GPUs and TPUs:** Training deep learning models can be computationally intensive, requiring powerful hardware like GPUs (Graphics Processing Units) or TPUs (Tensor Processing Units). These specialized hardware accelerators can significantly speed up training times compared to CPUs.
- **Cloud Computing:** Cloud computing platforms offer access to powerful GPUs and TPUs, making it easier for individuals and organizations to leverage deep learning without investing in expensive hardware.

Energy Consumption:

- **Environmental Impact:** Training deep learning models can be energy-intensive, raising concerns about environmental impact. Large-scale training operations can consume significant amounts of electricity.
- **Efficiency:** Efforts are being made to develop more energy-efficient deep learning algorithms and hardware to address these concerns.

In summary, computational resources play a crucial role in deep learning. Access to powerful hardware like GPUs or TPUs is essential for training large and complex models. Addressing the energy consumption associated with deep learning is also important to ensure sustainability and minimize environmental impact.

Interpretability

Interpretability is a critical aspect of deep learning, especially as these models are increasingly used in high-stakes applications.

Here's a more detailed explanation:

Black Box Problem:

- **Complexity:** Deep learning models can be highly complex, with millions of parameters and intricate connections. This complexity makes it difficult to understand how the model arrives at its decisions.
- **Lack of Transparency:** The black box nature of deep learning models can make it challenging to explain why the model made a particular prediction. This can be problematic in applications where understanding the reasoning behind a decision is important, such as medical diagnosis or financial decision-making.

Explainability:

- **Increased Demand:** There is a growing demand for explainable AI to increase trust and transparency in deep learning models. Explainable AI techniques can help users understand how the model works, identify potential biases, and detect errors.
- **Methods:** Several methods have been developed to improve the interpretability of deep learning models, including:

  - **Feature importance analysis:** Identifying the most important features that contribute to the model's predictions.
  - **Visualization techniques:** Visualizing the internal workings of the model to understand its decision-making process.
  - **Simplified models:** Creating simpler models that are easier to interpret while maintaining performance.

In summary, the black box problem is a significant challenge in deep learning. However, there is a growing emphasis on explainability to increase trust and transparency in AI systems. By developing techniques to interpret deep learning models, we can better understand how they work and ensure that they are used responsibly.

Overfitting and Underfitting

Overfitting and underfitting are two common challenges in machine learning, and finding the right balance between model complexity and data fit is crucial for building effective models.

Here's a more detailed explanation:

Overfitting:

- **Overly Complex Model:** Overfitting occurs when a model is too complex and learns the training data too well, leading to poor performance on new, unseen data.
- **Memorization:** The model may memorize the training data instead of learning general patterns.

Underfitting:

- **Insufficient Complexity:** Underfitting occurs when a model is too simple and cannot capture the underlying patterns in the data.
- **High Bias:** The model may have a high bias, meaning it makes strong assumptions about the data.

Balancing Complexity:

- **Model Selection:** Choosing the right model complexity is essential. A more complex model may be needed for complex tasks, but a simpler model may be sufficient for simpler tasks.
- **Cross-Validation:** Cross-validation can help to evaluate the model's performance on unseen data and identify the optimal level of complexity.

Regularization Techniques:

- **Dropout:** Dropout randomly drops out neurons during training, preventing the model from relying too heavily on any particular feature.
- **L1/L2 Regularization:** These techniques add a penalty term to the loss function, encouraging the model to have smaller weights. This can help to prevent overfitting by reducing the complexity of the model.

In summary, finding the right balance between model complexity and data fit is crucial for building effective machine learning models. Overfitting and underfitting are common challenges that can be addressed through careful model selection, cross-validation, and regularization techniques.

Ethical Considerations

Bias: Bias is a significant issue in deep learning, and it's crucial to address it to ensure fairness and equity in AI applications.

Here's a more detailed explanation:

- **Data Bias:** The data used to train deep learning models can contain biases that reflect societal biases. These biases can be present in various forms, such as gender, race, age, or socioeconomic status.
- **Perpetuating Bias:** If these biases are not addressed, the model may learn to perpetuate them, leading to unfair or discriminatory outcomes. For example, a facial recognition system trained on a dataset that primarily includes images of white people may struggle to accurately recognize people of color.

Addressing Bias:

- **Diverse Data:** Collecting diverse and representative data is essential to mitigate bias. This involves ensuring that the data includes individuals from various backgrounds and demographics.

- **Bias Detection and Mitigation:** Techniques like bias detection algorithms and fairness metrics can help identify and address biases in the data and model.
- **Ethical Considerations:** It's important to consider ethical implications when developing and deploying AI systems. Ensuring fairness and avoiding discrimination should be a priority.

In summary, bias is a significant challenge in deep learning, and addressing it is crucial for ensuring that AI systems are fair and equitable. By collecting diverse data, using bias detection techniques, and considering ethical implications, we can help mitigate bias and create more just and inclusive AI applications.

Privacy: Privacy is a major concern when dealing with large datasets, especially in the context of deep learning.

Here's a more detailed explanation:

- **Data Collection:** Collecting large amounts of data can raise privacy concerns, as it involves gathering personal information about individuals. This information can be sensitive and should be handled with care.
- **Data Usage:** How the data is used and shared can also raise privacy concerns. It's important to have clear policies and procedures in place to protect user privacy and prevent unauthorized access or misuse of data.
- **Regulations:** Many countries have strict data privacy laws, such as the General Data Protection Regulation (GDPR) in the European Union. Adhering to these regulations is crucial to avoid legal and reputational risks.

To address privacy concerns, organizations must implement robust data protection measures, obtain informed consent from individuals, and ensure transparency regarding data collection and usage. By prioritizing privacy, organizations can build trust with their users and avoid negative consequences.

Accountability: Accountability is a complex issue in the context of AI systems. Here's a more detailed explanation:

- **Black Box Problem:** Many AI systems, particularly deep learning models, are considered "black boxes" because it's difficult to understand how they make decisions. This can make it challenging to determine who is responsible for the actions or outcomes of these systems.
- **Human Involvement:** While AI systems can make decisions autonomously, they are often developed and deployed by humans. This raises questions about the extent to which humans should be held accountable for the actions of AI systems they create.
- **Ethical Considerations:** Ensuring accountability is crucial for addressing ethical concerns and preventing harmful consequences. It's important to have clear guidelines and regulations in place to establish who is responsible for the actions of AI systems and to hold individuals or organizations accountable for any negative outcomes.

Addressing accountability in AI is a complex issue that requires careful consideration of legal, ethical, and technical factors. As AI systems become more integrated into society, it will be essential to develop frameworks that ensure transparency, accountability, and fairness.

Future Directions

Addressing these challenges and limitations will be crucial for the continued development and adoption of deep learning. Future research areas include:

Data Efficiency:

- **Transfer Learning:** Leveraging knowledge from pre-trained models on large datasets to train new models on smaller datasets.

- **Meta-Learning**: Learning to learn, enabling models to adapt quickly to new tasks with limited data.
- **Data Augmentation**: Generating new training data from existing data to increase dataset size and diversity.

Interpretability:

- **Explainable AI (XAI)**: Developing techniques to make deep learning models more transparent and understandable.
- **Feature Importance Analysis**: Identifying the most important features that contribute to the model's predictions.
- **Visualization Techniques**: Visualizing the internal workings of deep learning models to understand their decision-making processes.

Fairness and Bias:

- **Diverse Datasets**: Ensuring that training data is diverse and representative to avoid biases.
- **Bias Detection and Mitigation**: Using techniques to identify and address biases in models.
- **Fairness Metrics**: Developing metrics to evaluate the fairness of AI systems.

Privacy and Security:

- **Federated Learning**: Training models on decentralized data to protect privacy.
- **Differential Privacy**: Adding noise to data to protect individual privacy while preserving statistical utility.
- **Secure Multi-Party Computation**: Enabling collaborative training of models without revealing sensitive data.

Hardware Efficiency:

- **Specialized Hardware**: Developing hardware specifically designed for deep learning, such as GPUs and TPUs.
- **Energy-Efficient Algorithms**: Optimizing algorithms and hardware to reduce energy consumption.
- **Neuromorphic Computing**: Exploring hardware inspired by the human brain for more efficient and energy-efficient computation.

By addressing these challenges, we can unlock the full potential of deep learning and create AI systems that are beneficial, responsible, and sustainable.

The Future of AI and Deep Learning

The future of AI and deep learning is incredibly promising, with the potential to revolutionize various industries and aspects of our lives. Here are some key trends and areas of focus:

Continued Advancements in Hardware

Continued advancements in hardware will play a crucial role in driving progress in AI and deep learning. Here's a more detailed explanation:

Specialized Hardware:

- **GPUs and TPUs**: Graphics Processing Units (GPUs) and Tensor Processing Units (TPUs) are specialized hardware designed to accelerate machine learning computations. These devices have significantly improved the speed and efficiency of training deep learning models.
- **NPUs**: Neural Processing Units (NPUs) are emerging as another promising hardware option for AI and deep learning. NPUs are specifically designed to accelerate neural network computations, offering potential performance gains over traditional GPUs and TPUs.

Edge Computing:

- **Real-time Processing:** Edge computing involves processing data closer to the source, rather than sending it to a central cloud. This can enable real-time processing and reduce latency, which is essential for applications like autonomous vehicles, IoT devices, and augmented reality.
- **Privacy and Security:** Edge computing can also improve privacy and security by reducing the amount of data that needs to be transmitted to the cloud.

In summary, advancements in specialized hardware and edge computing will continue to drive the development and adoption of AI and deep learning. These technologies will enable more efficient training, faster inference, and improved privacy and security, opening up new possibilities for AI applications across various industries.

Enhanced Explainability and Interpretability

Enhanced explainability and interpretability will be crucial for the continued development and adoption of AI systems. Here's a more detailed explanation:

Transparent Models:

- **Understanding Decision-Making:** Transparent models are designed to be easier to understand, allowing users to see how the model arrives at its decisions. This can help to build trust and accountability in AI systems.
- **Reduced Bias:** Transparent models can also help to identify and mitigate biases, as it is easier to understand how the model is making decisions and whether it is influenced by biases in the data.

Explainable AI Techniques:

- **Attention Mechanisms:** Attention mechanisms can be used to highlight the parts of the input data that are most important for the model's decision. This can help to explain the model's reasoning.

- **Feature Visualization:** Feature visualization techniques can be used to visualize the features that the model is focusing on. This can provide insights into the model's decision-making process.
- **Counterfactual Explanations:** Counterfactual explanations can help to understand how changes in the input data would affect the model's prediction. This can provide insights into the model's decision boundaries and help to identify potential biases.

By developing more transparent and explainable AI models, we can increase trust and accountability in AI systems, making them more widely adopted and accepted.

Ethical Considerations and Responsible AI

Bias and fairness: Addressing bias and ensuring fairness in AI systems will remain a crucial focus as AI continues to advance. Biases can be introduced into AI systems through various factors, including biased data, biased algorithms, and societal biases. These biases can have significant negative consequences, such as perpetuating discrimination, reinforcing stereotypes, and limiting opportunities. To address these issues, it is essential to collect diverse and representative data, develop unbiased algorithms, and promote transparency and explainability in AI systems. Additionally, fostering ethical guidelines and standards for AI development and deployment will help to ensure that AI is used responsibly and equitably. By actively addressing bias and ensuring fairness, we can help to harness the potential of AI for positive societal impact while minimizing its risks.

Privacy and security: Protecting privacy and data security will be essential as AI systems become more integrated into our lives. With the increasing collection and use of personal data, ensuring privacy and safeguarding sensitive information will be a top priority. As AI systems become capable of processing and analyzing vast amounts of data, it is crucial to implement robust data protection measures to prevent unauthorized access, data breaches, and misuse of personal information. This will require a combination of technical measures, such as encryption and access controls, and legal frameworks that establish clear guidelines for data collection, storage, and use. By prioritizing privacy and data security, we can build trust in AI systems and ensure that they are used responsibly and ethically.

Human-AI collaboration: Human-AI collaboration will be a key trend as AI systems become more sophisticated. Rather than replacing humans, AI can augment human capabilities and enhance productivity. By working together, humans and AI can leverage their respective strengths, with humans providing creativity, judgment, and domain expertise, while AI contributes computational power, data analysis, and automation. This collaborative approach can lead to more innovative solutions, improved decision-making, and enhanced efficiency across various industries. As AI continues to evolve, fostering effective human-AI collaboration will be essential for realizing the full potential of these technologies.

New Applications and Industries

Healthcare: AI and deep learning are revolutionizing healthcare in numerous ways. For example, AI can be used to analyze medical images, such as X-rays and MRIs, to detect diseases more accurately and efficiently. Additionally, AI-powered drug discovery platforms can accelerate the development of new treatments by analyzing vast amounts of data to identify potential drug candidates. Personalized medicine, which tailors treatments to individual patients based on their genetic makeup and other factors, is another area where AI is making significant strides.

Autonomous Systems: AI is a crucial component of autonomous systems, such as self-driving cars, drones, and robots. These systems rely on AI algorithms to perceive their surroundings, make decisions, and navigate safely. Autonomous vehicles, for instance, use AI to process sensor data, detect obstacles, and plan optimal routes.

Climate Change: AI can play a vital role in addressing climate change challenges. By analyzing large datasets of climate data, AI can help predict natural disasters, such as hurricanes and floods, and develop early warning systems. Additionally, AI can be used to optimize energy consumption and identify sustainable solutions for reducing greenhouse gas emissions.

Education: AI-powered personalized learning tools can revolutionize education by adapting to the individual needs and learning styles of students. These tools can provide personalized recommendations, offer targeted feedback, and identify areas where students may need additional support. This can help students achieve their full potential and improve overall learning outcomes.

Creativity: AI is also making significant strides in the field of creativity. AI-powered systems can generate art, music, and literature, often indistinguishable from human-created works. This has led to debates about the nature of creativity and the potential for AI to augment or even replace human creativity.

Challenges and Opportunities

Data quality and quantity: Data quality and quantity will continue to be significant challenges in the field of machine learning and artificial intelligence. While the availability of data has increased dramatically in recent years, ensuring data quality remains a crucial concern. Issues such as missing values, inconsistencies, biases, and privacy concerns can hinder the effectiveness of machine learning models. Additionally, the need for diverse and representative datasets is essential to prevent biases and ensure that models generalize well to different populations. As machine learning applications become more complex and widespread, addressing data quality and quantity challenges will be critical for developing reliable and ethical AI systems.

Talent and skills: Developing a skilled workforce with expertise in AI and deep learning will be essential for driving innovation and addressing the growing demand for AI applications. As AI continues to advance, there will be a need for professionals with a strong understanding of machine learning algorithms, data science techniques, and domain-specific knowledge. Investing in education and training programs to cultivate AI talent will be crucial for organizations to remain competitive and leverage the full potential of AI technologies. Additionally, fostering a collaborative and interdisciplinary environment will encourage the development of innovative AI solutions and address the ethical and societal implications of AI.

Ethical considerations: Ethical considerations will be crucial in the development and deployment of AI systems. As AI becomes increasingly integrated into our lives, it is essential to address concerns such as bias, fairness, privacy, and transparency. Ensuring that AI systems are developed and used responsibly will be critical for building trust and avoiding negative consequences. This will require collaboration between researchers, policymakers, and industry leaders to establish ethical guidelines and standards for AI development and deployment. Additionally, promoting diversity and inclusivity in the AI field will help to ensure that AI systems are developed with a variety of perspectives and avoid perpetuating biases.

The future of AI and deep learning is full of potential. By addressing the challenges and seizing the opportunities, we can create a future where AI is used to benefit society and improve people's lives.

NINE
KEY CONCEPTS

Deep Learning is a subset of machine learning that involves training artificial neural networks to learn from large amounts of data. It's inspired by the structure and function of the human brain and has achieved remarkable success in various applications.

Key components of a neural network:

- Neurons
- Weights and biases
- Activation functions
- Layers

Types of neural networks:

- Feedforward
- Convolutional
- Recurrent
- Autoencoders
- Generative Adversarial Networks (GANs)
- Transformers

Deep learning process:

- Data preparation and preprocessing

- Model training
- Model evaluation
- Hyperparameter tuning
- Addressing overfitting and underfitting

Ethical considerations in AI:

- Bias and fairness
- Privacy and data security
- Responsible AI development

Emerging deep learning techniques:

- Transformers
- Graph Neural Networks
- Generative Adversarial Networks with StyleGAN
- Neural Architecture Search
- Reinforcement Learning with Deep Neural Networks
- Federated Learning

Challenges and limitations of deep learning:

- Data requirements
- Computational resources
- Interpretability
- Ethical considerations

The future of AI and deep learning:

- Continued advancements in hardware
- Enhanced explainability and interpretability
- Ethical considerations and responsible AI
- New applications and industries

By understanding these key concepts and addressing the challenges, we can harness the power of deep learning to create innovative and beneficial AI applications.

Encouraging Further Exploration

To continue your journey and deepen your knowledge, consider the following suggestions:

Experiment with Different Frameworks and Techniques:

- **TensorFlow, PyTorch, and Keras:** These are popular deep learning frameworks that offer different strengths and features. Experimenting with each can help you understand their unique advantages and choose the best one for your projects.
- **Neural Network Architectures:** Explore different neural network architectures, such as convolutional neural networks (CNNs), recurrent neural networks (RNNs), and transformers, to understand their suitability for different tasks.
- **Hyperparameters and Regularization:** Experiment with different hyperparameters and regularization techniques to optimize model performance and prevent overfitting.

Work on Real-World Projects:

- **Hands-On Experience:** Applying your knowledge to practical projects is the best way to gain hands-on experience and see the impact of deep learning in action.
- **Problem-Solving:** Working on real-world projects will help you develop problem-solving skills and learn how to apply deep learning techniques to solve real-world problems.

Join Online Communities and Forums:

- **Learning from Others:** Connecting with other deep learning enthusiasts and experts can provide valuable insights, learning opportunities, and collaboration.

- **Sharing Knowledge:** Participating in online communities allows you to share your knowledge and experiences with others, contributing to the growth of the deep learning community.

Stay Updated with the Latest Research:

- **Research Papers:** Follow research papers and publications in the field of deep learning to stay updated on the latest advancements and techniques.
- **Conferences and Workshops:** Attend conferences and workshops to learn from experts and network with other researchers.
- **Online Courses:** Take online courses and tutorials to deepen your understanding of deep learning concepts and techniques.

Explore Specialized Areas:

- **Computer Vision:** Delve into computer vision tasks such as image classification, object detection, and image generation.
- **Natural Language Processing:** Explore natural language processing tasks such as machine translation, text summarization, and sentiment analysis.
- **Reinforcement Learning:** Explore reinforcement learning for tasks that involve decision-making and interaction with an environment.

By actively exploring and experimenting, you can continue to develop your deep learning skills and contribute to the advancement of this exciting field.

The Impact of Deep Learning on Society

Deep learning has the potential to significantly impact society in both positive and negative ways. Here are some of the key areas where deep learning is making a difference:

Positive Impacts

Healthcare:

- **Improved Medical Diagnosis:** Deep learning models can analyze medical images, such as X-rays and MRIs, with greater accuracy than human experts, leading to earlier detection and more effective treatment of diseases.
- **Drug Discovery:** AI is being used to accelerate drug discovery by analyzing vast amounts of data to identify potential drug candidates and predict their effectiveness.
- **Personalized Medicine:** Deep learning can enable personalized medicine by analyzing patient data to tailor treatments to individual needs, improving treatment outcomes.

Autonomous Systems:

- **Automation and Efficiency:** Deep learning is driving the development of autonomous vehicles, drones, and robots, which can automate tasks, improve efficiency, and reduce human error.
- **Safety:** Autonomous systems have the potential to improve safety in various industries, such as transportation and manufacturing.

Natural Language Processing:

- **Improved Communication:** Deep learning has made significant strides in natural language processing, enabling more accurate machine translation, chatbots, and voice assistants. This has improved communication and information access.

Creative Industries:

- **New Forms of Expression:** Deep learning is being used to generate creative content, such as art, music, and literature. This can lead to new forms of expression and inspire creativity.

Education:

- **Personalized Learning:** AI-powered personalized learning tools can help students learn at their own pace and improve educational outcomes by providing tailored instruction and feedback.
- **Accessibility:** AI can also be used to make education more accessible to students with disabilities, by providing assistive technologies and personalized learning experiences.

Negative Impacts
Job Displacement:

- **Automation of Tasks:** As AI systems become more capable, they can automate tasks that were previously performed by humans, leading to job displacement in certain industries.
- **Adapting to the Workforce:** It is crucial to invest in retraining and upskilling workers to prepare them for the changing job market and ensure a smooth transition.

Bias and Discrimination:

- **Perpetuating Bias:** If AI systems are trained on biased data, they can perpetuate existing biases and discrimination. This can have serious consequences, such as limiting opportunities for certain groups of people.
- **Addressing Bias:** It is essential to address bias in AI systems by using diverse datasets, developing fair algorithms, and promoting transparency and explainability.

Privacy Concerns:

- **Data Collection and Use:** The collection and use of large amounts of data for AI can raise privacy concerns. It is important to ensure that data is collected and used ethically and responsibly, and that individuals have control over their personal information.

Autonomous Weapons:

- **Ethical Concerns:** The development of autonomous weapons raises serious ethical concerns, such as the potential for misuse and the loss of human control.
- **International Regulation:** It is essential to develop international regulations and guidelines to prevent the development and use of autonomous weapons in a harmful manner.

Overall Impact:

The impact of deep learning on society is complex and multifaceted. While it has the potential to bring significant benefits, it is essential to address the challenges and risks associated with its development and deployment. By developing and using AI responsibly, we can harness its power to create a better future for all.

TEN

CONCLUSION

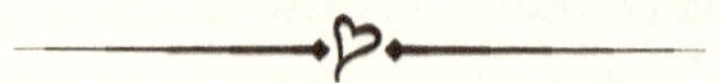

In our exploration of Unleashing the Machine Mind, we've delved into the fascinating realm of deep learning, unraveling the intricate concepts that underpin its revolutionary capabilities. From understanding the architecture of neural networks, inspired by the human brain, to grasping the power of backpropagation, the algorithm that allows neural networks to learn, we've witnessed the transformative potential of deep learning in various domains. Deep learning has enabled machines to recognize patterns in images and videos with unprecedented accuracy, surpassing human capabilities in tasks like image classification and object detection. It has revolutionized natural language processing, enabling machines to understand and generate human language, from translating texts to creating creative writing. In the realm of healthcare, deep learning has shown promise in diagnosing diseases, analyzing medical images, and even developing new drug treatments. Beyond these applications, deep learning is also driving advancements in fields like autonomous vehicles, robotics, and financial technology. As we continue to advance our understanding and applications of deep learning, we can anticipate even more groundbreaking developments that will shape our future in exciting and unimaginable ways. The possibilities are endless, and the journey of unleashing the machine mind has only just begun.

ELEVEN

REFERENCES

1. Patra, S. (2024). Unleashing the Power: Exploring Deep Learning Architecture for Cutting-Edge AI Solutions. In *Deep Learning Concepts in Operations Research* (pp. 44-55). Auerbach Publications.

2. Madakam, S., Uchiya, T., Mark, S., & Lurie, Y. (2022). Artificial intelligence, machine learning and deep learning (literature: review and metrics). *Asia-Pacific Journal of Management Research and Innovation, 18*(1-2), 7-23.

3. Kurni, M., Mohammed, M. S., & Srinivasa, K. G. (2023). Ethics of Artificial Intelligence in Education. In *A Beginner's Guide to Introduce Artificial Intelligence in Teaching and Learning* (pp. 213-229). Cham: Springer International Publishing.

4. Lowndes, A. B. (2015). *Deep Learning with GPU Technology for Image & Feature Recognition* (Doctoral dissertation, Tesis de Grado]. University of Leeds).

5. Imamverdiyev, Y., & Abdullayeva, F. (2018). Deep learning method for denial of service attack detection based on restricted boltzmann machine. *Big data, 6*(2), 159-169.

6. Liu, W., Wang, Z., Liu, X., Zeng, N., Liu, Y., & Alsaadi, F. E. (2017). A survey of deep neural network architectures and their applications. *Neurocomputing, 234*, 11-26.

7. Goodfellow, I. (2016). Deep learning.

8. Deng, L., & Yu, D. (2014). Deep learning: methods and applications. *Foundations and trends® in signal processing, 7*(3–4), 197-387.

9. Abadi M, Barham P, Chen J, Chen Z, Davis A, Dean J, Devin Ma, Ghemawat S, Irving G, Isard M, et al. Tensorflow: a system for large-scale machine learning. In: 12th {USENIX} Symposium on operating systems design and implementation ({OSDI} 16), 2016; p. 265–283.

10. Clark, D. (2024). *Artificial Intelligence for Learning: Using AI and Generative AI to Support Learner Development.* Kogan Page Publishers.

11. Ahmed, A. A., Alsharif, A., & Khaleel, M. Arti icial Intelligence.

12. Mangtani, A. J. (2024). Science of Learning and Its Theories. In *Instructional Design Unleashed: Unlocking Professional Learning Potential with UX, Agile and AI Methods* (pp. 29-79). Berkeley, CA: Apress.

13. Holmes, W., & Littlejohn, A. (2024). Artificial intelligence for professional learning. In *Handbook of Artificial Intelligence at Work* (pp. 191-211). Edward Elgar Publishing.

14. Lanham, M., & Lanham, M. (2021). The Basics of Deep Learning. *Generating a New Reality: From Autoencoders and Adversarial Networks to Deepfakes,* 1-34.

15. Eklöf, J., Hamelryck, T., Last, C., Grima, A., & Snis, U. L. (2023). Abstraction, mimesis and the evolution of deep learning. *Ai & Society,* 1-9.

16. Howard, D., & Werdelin, J. (2021). *The Beginner's Guide to Cooperative Learning: Make your learners your main teaching resource.* Crown House Publishing Ltd.

17. Ribeiro, J. (2021). *AI in 2020: A Year writing about Artificial Intelligence.* Jair Ribeiro.

18. Sadiku, M. N., Musa, S. M., & Chukwu, U. C. (2022). *Artificial intelligence in education.* iUniverse.

19. Fahad, M., Basri, T., Hamza, M. A., Faisal, S., Akbar, A., Haider, U., & Hajjami, S. E. (2024). The Benefits and Risks of Artificial General Intelligence (AGI). In *Artificial General Intelligence (AGI)*

Security: Smart Applications and Sustainable Technologies (pp. 27-52). Singapore: Springer Nature Singapore.

20. Yu, S., & Lu, Y. (2021). *An introduction to artificial intelligence in education*. Singapore: Springer.